C000247124

Bonnie Prince Charlie:
Truth or Lies?

Bonnie Prince Charlie: Truth or Lies?

RODERICK GRAHAM

SAINT ANDREW PRESS
Edinburgh

First published in 2014 by
SAINT ANDREW PRESS
121 George Street
Edinburgh EH2 4YN

Copyright © Roderick Graham 2014

ISBN 978-0-86153-783-9

All rights reserved. No part of this publication may be reproduced or transmitted
in any form or by any means, electronic or mechanical, including photocopy,
recording, or information storage and retrieval system, without permission in
writing from the publisher. This book is sold subject to the condition that it shall
not, by way of trade or otherwise, be lent, resold, hired out or otherwise circulated
without the publisher's prior consent.

The opinions expressed in this book are those of the author and do not necessarily
reflect those of the publisher.

The right of Roderick Graham to be identified as author of this work has been
asserted in accordance with the Copyright, Designs and Patents Act 1988.

British Library Cataloguing in Publication Data
A catalogue record for this book is available from the British Library.

It is the publisher's policy to only use papers that are natural and recyclable and
that have been manufactured from timber grown in renewable, properly managed
forests. All of the manufacturing processes of the papers are expected to conform to
the environmental regulations of the country of origin.

Typeset by Regent Typesetting
Printed and bound by ScandBook AB Sweden

Contents

As usual this book is dedicated to Fiona, my wife, who never complains about being disturbed when I tell her something I had forgotten.

Preface

The most charismatic man in Scottish history was Charles Edward Louis Casimir Silvester Severino Maria Stuart or 'Bonnie Prince Charlie'. His heroic figure has graced more shortbread tins than there are pictures of Shakespeare on tea-towels in Stratford-upon-Avon. His life was a heady mixture of adventure and legend. Some 'truths' are merely legends which have gained credence by repetition – and some of the most apparently fanciful events are true occurrences.

This book poses a series of questions about the various myths surrounding this fascinating character and, in answering them, explains his true motives for such a romantic, if finally disastrous, career.

Royal Houses

Great Britain

THE HOUSE OF STUART

JAMES VI AND I
1603–25

CHARLES I
1625–49

THE COMMONWEALTH
1649–60

THE HOUSE OF STUART (contd)

CHARLES II
1660–85

JAMES VII and II
1685–88 (exiled) died 1701

THE HOUSE OF ORANGE

WILLIAM III
1688–1702

THE HOUSE OF STUART (contd)

ANNE
1702–14

THE HOUSE OF HANOVER

GEORGE I
1714–27

GEORGE II
1727–60

GEORGE III
1760–1820

THE HOUSE OF STUART IN EXILE

JAMES III
1688–1766

CHARLES EDWARD
1720–88

France

HOUSE OF BOURBON

LOUIS XIV
1643–1715

LOUIS XV
1715–74

LOUIS XVI
1774–92

THE PAPACY

CLEMENT XI
1700–21

INNOCENT XIII
1721–24

BENEDICT XIII
1724–30

CLEMENT XII
1730–40

BENEDICT XIV
1740–58

CLEMENT XIII
1758–69

CLEMENT XIV
1769–74

PIUS VI
1775–99

A Brief Timeline

10 June 1688	Birth of James III
1701	James II dies. James III is now the Old Pretender
31 December 1720	Birth of Charles Edward Louis Casimir Silvester Severino Maria
1725	Birth of Charles's brother, Henry
August 1745	Charles lands at Moidart with the Seven Men
19 August 1745	Raises the standard at Glenfinnan
4 September 1745	Declares his father King of Great Britain at Perth
17 September 1745	Enters Edinburgh
21 September 1745	Wins victory at Prestonpans
8 November 1745	Marches into England
5 December 1745	'Black Friday', the day Charles starts to return from Derby

20 December 1745	Arrives back in Glasgow
17 January 1746	Trounces 'Hangman' Hawley at Falkirk
15/16 April 1746	Defeated at Culloden
21 June 1746	Meets Flora MacDonald
10 October 1746	Arrives back in France
10 December 1748	Expelled from France
1750	Converts to the Church of England
1753	Daughter Charlotte is born
1 January 1766	James III dies
1772	Married to Louise de Stolberg as a Catholic
30 January 1788	Dies in Rome

Principal Characters

Alfieri, Count Vittorio   Louise de Stolberg's lover

Balhaldy, MacGregor of   Charles's ambassador to Paris

Bouillon, Duc de   Charles's protector in France

Bourk (Burke), Edward   A sedan-chair porter and Charles's guide in the flight from the Highlands

Bradstreet, Dudley   A Hanoverian double agent

Choiseul, Duc de   War Minister to Louis XV

Cope, Sir John   A Hanoverian general

Cumberland, William Augustus   Duke and second son of George II, commander of the army in Scotland

D'Eguilles, Marquis   A French envoy

Elibank, Alexander Murray of   English Jacobite and conspirator

Forbes, Duncan   Lord President of the Court of Session

Gordon, John, Laird of Glenbucket   A loyal supporter from the North-East

Goring, Sir Henry   A close supporter and sometime agent

Guémène, Princesse de   Marie de Montbazon's mother-in-law

Hamilton, Sir William   British ambassador in Naples

Hawley, Henry   Lieutenant-General of the Hanoverian army, a military sadist nicknamed 'Hangman' Hawley

Hume, David   Scottish historian and philosopher who met Charles in strange circumstances

Kelly, George   One of the Seven Men of Moidart, he was a malign influence and an architect of the disaster at Culloden

Ligonier, Lord John   Hanoverian commander

Lochiel, Donald Cameron of   One of Charles's most loyal supporters

Loudoun, Lord   Hanoverian commander of the Inverness garrison

Louis XV   King of France and Charles's host from 1746 to 1748

Lovat, Lord, Simon Fraser   A nobleman best known for his varying loyalty

Macdonald, Aeneas   One of the Seven Men of Moidart

MacDonald, Flora   Daughter of Ranald MacDonald, she spent a few days guiding Charles, disguised as 'Betty Burke', through the Hebrides

Macdonald, John   One of the Seven Men of Moidart

MacDonald of Boisdale   A Skye chieftain opposed to Charles

MacDonald of Sleat   A Skye chieftain opposed to Charles

Mackintosh, Lord Angus   Husband to Lady Anne and of dubious loyalty

Mackintosh, Lady Anne   Nicknamed 'Colonel Anne', a staunch supporter who organised the 'Rout of Moy'

Macleod, Norman   A Skye chieftain opposed to Charles

Macpherson, Cluny   A loyal supporter offering Charles refuge in 'Cluny's Cage', his secret hideaway

Mar, John, Earl of   Nicknamed 'Bobbing John', he supported James in the 1715 rising but subsequently changed sides

Montbazon, Marie de   Charles's first mistress, whom he treated abominably

Montesquieu, Charles-Louis de   French philosopher and acquaintance of Charles

Murray, Lord George   Lieutenant-General of the Jacobite army

Murray, James, Earl of Dunbar   Charles's governor as a boy

Murray of Broughton   Charles's officer in charge of provisions

Newcastle, Lord   Prime Minister of Britain

O'Sullivan, John   One of the Seven Men of Moidart, an evil influence on Charles

Petrovna, Elizabeth   Czarina of Russia, Charles proposed marriage to her

Primrose, Lady   An English Jacobite

Puysieux   Foreign minister to Louis XV

Richelieu, Duc de   French nobleman, military commander and libertine

Saxe, Maurice   Marshal, French military commander

Sheridan, Thomas   One of the Seven Men of Moidart, and Charles's under-governor

Sobieska, Clementina   Charles's mother, a Polish princess, granddaughter of Jan Sobieski who saved Vienna from the Turks

Stewart, John Roy   A Jacobite mercenary commander of the Edinburgh regiment

Stolberg, Louise de   A German princess whom Charles married in 1772

Strickland, Francis   One of the Seven Men of Moidart

Stuart, Charlotte   Charles's illegitimate daughter, born in 1753

Stuart, Henry   Charles's younger brother, Bishop of Frascati and a cardinal

Stuart, James   Father to Charles, Pretender to the throne of Great Britain, his very legitimacy was in doubt thanks to the scandal of the warming pan

Talmont, Princesse de   Charles's second mistress

Tullibardine, William   One of the Seven Men of Moidart

Wade, George   Hanoverian general

Walkinshaw, Clementina   Niece to Hugh Paterson, nursed Charles in 1746 and in 1753 bore him a daughter

Williams Wynn, Sir Watkin   A hoped-for Welsh Jacobite who never materialised

Chapter 1

He intended to take the throne as Charles III

On 23 July 1745 the 24-year-old Charles Edward Louis Casimir Silvester Severino Maria Stuart landed on the tiny island of Eriskay in the remote Outer Hebrides, some 60 miles west of the Scottish mainland. The great Skye chiefs, Norman Macleod and Alexander MacDonald of Sleat, thought his purpose in coming to Scotland was doomed and refused to join him. Alexander MacDonald of Boisdale strongly advised him to go home. He replied, 'I am come home', and a legend was born.

The legend that was Bonnie Prince Charlie

Before landing, an eagle was seen hovering above the ship, viewed as a strong omen of success to the superstitious Highlanders. Another legend is that seeds of pink convolvulus, a seed foreign to Scotland, fell from Charles's jacket pocket and took root. Even by meeting Charles, the Skye chiefs had placed themselves outside the law, since in 1743 Parliament had passed an Act of Attainder whereby Charles, his brother Henry and any offspring of theirs were outlawed.

A few days later, in August 1745, after the treacherous sea crossing, Prince Charles at last set foot on the Scottish mainland at Moidart on the north-west coast. He was dressed as an English clergyman and accompanied not by an army but by the 'Seven Men of Moidart', who are famous only for the smallness of their number. They were William Tullibardine, Francis Strickland, Thomas Sheridan, George Kelly, John Macdonald, Aeneas Macdonald and John O'Sullivan.

He had brought only these seven, mainly Irish, supporters with him, so what were his intentions and what could he hope to achieve? His openly declared aim was to bring about the restoration of the Stuart dynasty, exiled in 1701, and to see his father, James III, taking the British throne as King of Great Britain. Reasonably certain that his father would never want to leave his present home at the Palazzo Muti in Rome, he would declare himself Regent until his father's death – his father died in 1766 – when he would be crowned as Charles III.

We must look at his legal right to claim the throne of a country he had only just seen for the first time. The legitimacy of the Stuarts was never in doubt, and the Prince could trace his ancestry back for over 400 years in a direct line to Robert the Bruce. However, it was a sorry tale of deaths and deceit and is swiftly told.

The dynasty started when Marjorie Bruce, daughter of Robert I, married Walter the Steward and in 1316 gave birth to Robert Stewart, crowned in 1371 as Robert II. His son, Robert III, in 1394 fathered James I who was stabbed to death by his own nobles in a castle privy in 1437. James

II had no better luck when, in 1460, he was inspecting a cannon during the siege of Roxburgh in the Scottish borders. The cannon exploded, killing him instantly. His son was the unpopular James III whose nobles rose against him during the Battle of Sauchieburn, near Stirling. The chronicle tells us simply that the king 'happenit to be slain'. His son, who has been suspected of the killing, succeeded as James IV in 1488, establishing a glittering Renaissance court only to die himself at the Battle of Flodden in 1513. He was followed by James V, who had the distinction of dying in his bed, albeit on hearing the bad news that his French-born queen had given birth to a girl. She was Mary, Queen of Scots, who was beheaded on suspicion of having agreed to a plot to assassinate Elizabeth Tudor, although on Elizabeth's death in 1603 Mary's son became James VI and I, the king of the newly named Great Britain. The spelling of the name changed to Stuart about this time, and James reigned in comparative peace due to a series of uneasy compromises with the nascent Parliament which showed signs of flexing its financial muscles. Stuart kings were not used to Parliament putting a brake on their ambitions, since they firmly believed that they ruled by the divine right granted to them by God at their coronation.

Sadly, what constitutional compromises had existed started to collapse when James died and his son came to the throne as Charles I. The conflict between King and Parliament led to the Civil War and the execution of Charles I in 1649. His son, Charles II, was defeated at the Battle of Worcester and fled into exile in Europe, returning in 1660 as 'the Merry Monarch' while agreeing to accord more power to Parliament and faithfully to uphold the Protestant faith.

The struggle for mastery between King and Parliament continued, taking on a religious note by Charles's marriage to Catherine of Braganza, a Portuguese princess and a devout Catholic. Charles was wrongly suspected of having secretly converted to Catholicism and of having sympathies with Louis XIV of France. He managed to retain popular support by having two principal mistresses. One, Louise de Kerouaille, later Duchess of Portsmouth, was a French Catholic suspected, probably justifiably, of being a spy for Louis XIV. The other official mistress was Nell Gwynne, who was sexually more adept and, more practically, overtly Protestant. She endeared herself to the mob when, having had her coach overturned, she rose from the wreckage to declare with pride, 'Leave me alone, you fools! I'm the English whore!'

Charles died in 1685 after what seems to have been a series of strokes combined with a collapse of his kidneys. He was bled and blistered, and red-hot irons were applied to his shaven head and feet, while a total of 58 different drugs were administered, most of them poisonous. Charles apologised to his baffled tormentors for 'being so long a time a-dying', then secretly admitted Father Huddlestone, a Catholic priest, who received him into the Catholic faith, heard his confession and gave him absolution.

Charles was succeeded by his brother James VII and II, and with this accession of a devout Catholic the ill-fated Stuart dynasty started to unravel seriously.

James was 52 years old and the years of standing in his brother's shadow had exacerbated the differences between the two men. Where Charles had been flexible and willing to accept the views of others, James was rigidly dogmatic and acted solely on his own desires – a dangerous trait, which he passed on to his grandson, Prince Charles. In his book on Hollywood, *Adventures in the Screen Trade*, William Goldman tells us that the mark of a true star is that, from rising to sleeping, they know that no one will disagree with them or deny them anything. This was an unfortunate character flaw of most of the Stuarts, and Prince Charles was a prime example of this inherent arrogance.

However, the most dangerous aspect of James's self-centredness was his overt, even flagrant Catholicism, and within a fortnight of his accession he publicly celebrated Mass in the Chapel Royal at Whitehall.

More immediately, he had to deal with a threat to his very sovereignty when on 11 June 1685 the Duke of Monmouth landed with about 150 followers at Lyme Regis in Dorset, claiming to be the true King of Britain. Monmouth was the 36-year-old illegitimate son of Charles II. Although popular in the country he had had to flee to the Netherlands as a result of his allegiance to the Roman Church. He was proclaimed James II at Taunton and he gained support from the miners and weavers of the West Country. William of Orange sent him three regiments of Scots who had been in his service in the Netherlands, but his path was blocked by the royal forces which he attempted to surprise at Sedgemoor. His men were slaughtered in the marshy land and he was captured hiding waist-deep in a flooded ditch. He was taken to London and beheaded, while vengeance fell on the West Country in the form of Judge Jeffreys with his 'Bloody Assizes', which indiscriminately meted out death or transportation to all and sundry.

At the same time the Duke of Argyll attempted to rise in Scotland in support of Monmouth, but his revolt was a dismal failure and he met a less bloody version of Monmouth's fate.

Both of these revolts gave James the excuse to strengthen the army and to establish a standing army in time of peace. To ensure its loyalty, he re-officered the army with Catholic – often Irish – officers. He spread the influence of Rome to Oxford and Cambridge, and Catholic masters of colleges began to be appointed. The civil administration was also reformed with a preponderance of Catholics. This was contrary to the Test Acts, whereby anyone taking public office had to swear fidelity to the Anglican Church, but James simply used the royal prerogative to ride roughshod over the law.

These events coincided with Louis XIV of France revoking the Edict of Nantes in 1685, which had allowed freedom of worship to Protestants, and Parliament became seriously worried that James's behaviour would allow similar breaks with the supremacy of Protestantism. Parliament even offered him a grant of £700,000 to ensure religious toleration, which they could see diminishing to pre-Reformation limits, but James refused the grant and prorogued Parliament.

Domestically, James was not without troubles, since he had been married to Mary of Modena, an Italian-born Catholic, for 15 years. She had borne five daughters and one son, all of whom had died in infancy, but now at the age of 30, advanced for the time, she announced that she was again pregnant. Catholics claimed her pregnancy as a miracle while Protestants were certain it was a sham. However, on 1 July 1688 she was delivered of a son. The rumour mill continued to turn and a bizarre tale was spread that a new-born baby was smuggled into the royal birthing chamber in a warming pan and slid secretly into the queen's bed. In any case, the child was christened James Francis Edward and would become Prince Charles Edward's father as James III, or the 'Old Pretender'. Thus, warming pan or no – and it is a very fanciful calumny – James Francis's christening and upbringing legitimised him and his sons.

Parliament, however, was now bitterly opposed to James II's high-handed methods and flagrant Catholicism. It was not unduly paranoid on their part to see the effective government of the country, the Civil Service and the military, being totally dominated by the king's co-religionist cronies. Parliament tried to avoid outright opposition, with memories of the Civil War only 40 years previously, and any means of replacing James, more or less constitutionally, were examined with some care.

James's elder sister Mary had married William II, Prince of Orange, a demonstrably Protestant Dutchman. Even more conveniently, his son, William III of Orange, had married another Mary, a daughter of James II by a first marriage. James's earlier bride, Anne, had died in 1671, but there were currently strong marital links with adjacent Protestant royalty, albeit of a nation with which England had recently been involved in a violent trade war, ending only in 1678.

Informal approaches were made to William, who diplomatically responded saying that he would not come to England unless formally invited. In other words, he would not come as a usurper. Therefore in July 1688 Arthur Herbert, the ex-vice-admiral of England, sailed for the Netherlands with such an invitation signed by seven great magnates.

James had now clearly lost all support domestically, and he asked for naval help from Louis XIV. Since Louis had no effective fleet this was not forthcoming, and James received instead a promise that any attack on England would be regarded by Louis as an attack on France. The promise was meaningless since Louis knew very well not only what was being planned but also that he could easily wriggle out of any inconvenient commitment.

Even a man of James's monumental arrogant stupidity could see that he had created a situation of complete hostility with his Parliament, and he attempted to summon it again, presumably to make amends. He restored charters to cities where they had been suspended, removed some of the more bigoted lords-lieutenant, issued a general pardon and restored the Protestant fellows of Magdalen.

But it was all too late, as on 4 November 1688 William of Orange's fleet arrived safely at Torbay in Devon, and within 11 days the disembarkation, which had been unopposed, was complete. William was the first foreign invader since his Norman namesake had arrived in 1066. A fortnight later William's army was at Salisbury, with remarkably few casualties since William wisely avoided any conflict with the royal forces which could lose him popular sympathy.

In December the infant James was sent to Portsmouth, then hastily taken back to London.

Foolishly, James disbanded the royal army and sowed bitter discontent by refusing to pay them, while the peers met in London's Guildhall and sent a message to William assuring him that they would hold London until his arrival. The peers decided that a forced abdication would be invalid but that James must leave London, and so at 3 o'clock in the morning of 21 December James fled to Sheerness where a ship was waiting for the tide. Before the tide turned he was seized by local fishermen and sent back to London. The Stuarts seemed to be cursed with comic ineptitude.

Having failed even to flee his kingdom, he was now allowed to sail openly for Rochester then across the English Channel to France, and on 25 December 1688 he celebrated Christmas Mass at Ambleteuse, a village between Calais and Boulogne. Shortly afterwards, James, his family and a small court were established as the guests of Louis XIV at St Germain-en-Laye to the north of Paris.

James Stuart had fled without the use of force and without negotiation with Parliament. Contrary to what is often claimed, he had signed no articles of abdication, valid or not, and in accordance with the current law he was still the rightful King of Great Britain. The machinery for governing the country was now in a complete mess, and a fresh parliament was elected. But since this had not been summoned by the king and was therefore illegal, it called itself a 'convention', although the difference is entirely semantic. The Whig members claimed that the king had *de facto* abdicated, if not *de jure*. In the interests of expediency these troublesome questions were brushed aside in favour of offering the crown to William, with the proviso that James's daughter, Anne, should succeed him. A Declaration of Rights was drawn up – soon to be a Bill of Rights – limiting the royal power in various ways, and by 23 February 1689 William agreed to accept the throne.

The Glorious Revolution – sometimes called the Bloodless Revolution – which was not in fact a revolution at all, seemed, from London's point of view, to be complete, but this was far from the truth.

In Scotland there had been strong objections to James's introduction of Catholics to posts of power, and riots had taken place in Edinburgh. The Duke of Argyll had risen in favour of Monmouth, for which he was summarily hanged. The arrival of Protestant William was greeted with enthusiasm, and in Edinburgh the Catholic chapel at Holyrood Palace was wrecked. In the south-west several Episcopalian ministers were 'rabbled', which is to say they were turned out of their homes and left to fend for themselves in a hostile country. Support for James was strongest in the Highlands, where opposition united under Viscount Dundee (Graham of Claverhouse) and came to meet the loyal army at Killiecrankie on 27 July 1689. These supporters of James, or 'Jacobites', were victorious but Dundee was killed. However, the Jacobites then suffered defeats at Dunkeld and Cromdale, and by May 1690 the first Jacobite rising was over and James's supporters vanished back into their glens.

Their loyalty was tested when they sought peace and were required to sign an oath of loyalty to William. When Macdonald of Glencoe was late in signing, John Dalrymple of Stair saw an opportunity to make an example and, probably without royal consent, authorised Campbell of Glenlyon to punish the tardy clansmen. The result was the Massacre of Glencoe in February 1692, when the Campbells, who had been guests of the Macdonalds in Glencoe, rose against their hosts in the night and slaughtered 33 men, two women and two children.

This example of internecine Highland warfare casts doubt

over the popular belief that the Jacobite risings were Highland versus Lowland. Instead the quarrel was more deeply
between the traditional Tory beliefs in wealth based on land-
holding and feudal loyalty in the Highlands, in contrast to
the Whig policy of increase in wealth from rising capitalism
in the Lowlands. It is a gross simplification to see the Jacobite
movement simply in terms of Highland versus Lowland or of
Protestant English versus Catholic Scottish. The differences
were far wider and more complex than a mere geographical
separation.

The situation in Ireland was, for once, much simpler.
James had re-officered the army with Catholics, and there
were French regiments under the command of the Earl of
Tyrconnel. James had recently appointed Tyrconnel as Viceroy,
so Ireland now represented a Catholic hegemony on William's
doorstep. Totally ignoring what he had sworn to in the treaty
of Ryswick, when he had accepted William as King of Great
Britain, Louis XIV saw this as a chance to separate Ireland from
England, strongly encouraging the exiled James's discontent.
On 2 March 1689 James duly invaded Ireland.

The first move was against Londonderry, but Louis had
sent no military supplies capable of breaking a siege, and so
both sides settled in for a long and punishing campaign of
105 days. Despairing of the slow progress of the indecisive
local skirmishes, William himself landed to take command
on 24 June 1690. James had cut off William's route to Dublin
and his forces were dug in across the River Boyne a few miles
north of the capital. The attack came on 11 July and was
a decisive victory for William. By August 1690 James was
back in France. The Catholic defeat at the Battle of the Boyne

is still remembered by Protestant, or 'Orange', supporters in commemorative marches.

In London William and Mary had been crowned in April 1689, and the 'convention', which had ruled in place of a royally summoned Parliament, formally declared itself a legal Parliament. James saw out his days in lonely exile at La Trappe in France, and in England the paranoid suspicion of Jacobite plots fell in intensity. Then in 1701 James died and his three-year-old son was proclaimed as James III, with the full endorsement of Louis XIV. Discounting the possibility that the infant might be raised as a Protestant, William's Parliament realised that, although the Stuart horse had well and truly bolted, they had better fit secure locks on the stable door.

This was the Act of Settlement of 1701, which codified the royal succession. William and Mary were childless and likely to remain so. Thus the crown would pass to Anne Stuart, Mary's sister. Anne was 36 years old, had been married for 18 years and had produced no living children. But James VI and I's granddaughter Sofia was married to the Elector of Hanover, a devout Protestant, and she had borne a healthy son, George. On Anne's death (in 1714) he would become King George I, and by this Act the House of Hanover would rule Great Britain.

In March 1702 this system went into effect when William's horse stumbled on a molehill, throwing the king, who never recovered from the fall, and Anne became queen. Romantic crypto-Jacobites still drink a toast to 'the little gentleman in the black velvet waistcoat'. They also pass their spirit glasses across their water glass before drinking the loyal toast. It thus becomes a toast to 'the king across the water'.

The Act of Settlement made many other conditions, most important of which was that no Catholic, or any person married to a Catholic, could succeed to the British throne, effectively putting an end to any hope of the restoration of the Stuarts.

James III, the 'Old Pretender', was three years old and in exile. He would marry a rich Polish aristocrat in 1719 and they would have a child in 1720. This child was Charles Edward Stuart, 'Bonnie Prince Charlie' or the 'Young Pretender'.

To restore the Stuarts, James or Charles would not only have to oust the reigning monarch, presumably by military force, but also persuade Parliament to repeal the Act of Settlement. This task would fall to Charles Edward by proclaiming his father as king and himself as regent. His next move could wait until James III's death placed him upon the throne. The dynastic right to rule undoubtedly lay with James III and his son, but Parliament had put almost insuperable difficulties in the way. Whether this situation would continue, only history would tell. After all, surely Charles Edward Stuart was 'the man born to be king!' as Charles III.

Chapter 2

He was the slave of his father's ambition

This was absolutely untrue, since it has been impossible to identify ambition as a trait in James III's character. In fact some unkind commentators claim that it has been impossible to identify any trace of character in James's personality.

The reasons for this are not hard to find. James was orphaned at three years of age, and the conditions of his childhood were such as to sow the seeds of low self-esteem. He must have been aware that his very existence was doubted, since the extravagant calumny of the warming pan must have affected him in some way, although it was always difficult to find any trace of passion in him. Then an immersion in a foreign country, with the almost immediate absence of his father, returning only after the Battle of the Boyne as a defeated man, hardly made the ideal circumstances for the most stable of infancies, even for a royal child inured to long paternal absences.

The hospitality of Louis XIV had been stretched too far when in 1713 James and his tiny court were forced to leave St Germain-en-Laye and he would commence his life as 'Jamie the Rover', seeking help and hospitality where he could find it. James even hired himself out as a mercenary soldier on Louis's side at the Battle of Malplaquet on 11 September 1709.

He was the opposite of his father James II. Whereas James II was intransigent and dogmatic, his son was all too compliant. James II sought out differences in order to oppose them, while James III would avoid all controversy. In this policy of 'quietism' he was a follower of the French philosopher Fenelon, Bishop of Cambrai. Fenelon was a man who 'needs know the cause and the reason of everything that is proposed to him'. He advocated 'humility in everything', which 'puts us in the place which belongs to us while knowledge puffeth us up'. These precepts of quiet ignorance and acceptance sat ill on the shoulders of an exiled king. James was exhorted never to be an apostle but to be a good king without distinction. He also had the neurasthenic's horror of making decisions and, when he was forced to make them, frequently fell ill with crippling fevers, often diagnosed as the quartan ague, a fever recurring every fourth day for an unspecified period. This was a trait he passed on to his son, in that Charles, when thwarted, often took to his bed. Both men lacked father figures, and since they had in reality no money they were doomed to lead second-hand lives dependent on the hospitality of others and subject to their acceptance of their hosts' views.

Finding this hospitality first at Commercy in Lorraine, where his widowed mother, Mary of Modena, held her court a mere 100 miles from Paris, and then at Avignon and Urbino, all places in the sovereignty of the papacy, James finally settled in the Palazzo Muti in Rome in 1710 under the somewhat grudging protection of Pope Clement XI.

For all that the building held the name of 'palazzo', it was a rather drab courtyard opposite the church of SS Apostoli near the Piazza Navona in central Rome, and James's exiled court did nothing to relieve the gloom. An army of hangers-on designed spurious orders and issued meaningless edicts.

The failure of James's campaign in Ireland had stalled the Jacobite cause and James was no inspiring leader to rekindle the flame. In England the Jacobite cause attached itself more to political disaffection with the Whigs than to a restoration of the Stuarts, and flourished more around claret and brandy bottles than taking any real military form. There was a slight acceleration in purpose when the death of Queen Anne inspired the Dean of Westminster and Bishop of Rochester, Francis Atterbury, to declare James III as rightful king from the steps of the Royal Exchange. Atterbury was not on this occasion accompanied by his ally and closet Jacobite, Henry Bolingbroke, one of Queen Anne's ministers, who felt that this was not the time for a Jacobite challenge to the Hanoverian succession. This was a view shared by the Duke of Marlborough, who had been holding a pointless correspondence with James – pointless since the great warrior's offer of help was greeted with responses that were, at best, lukewarm.

The German-speaking George I arrived in Britain in September 1714. George was keen to fill his government with more Whigs, and Atterbury predictably spent a brief spell in the Tower of London. Bolingbroke left for France while Marlborough managed to retain his position as captain-general.

In Paris there was a renewed enthusiasm among the romantically inclined Jacobites for the restoration of James, and in England George's unpopularity gave a greater focus to disaffected statesmen such as the Duke of Ormonde, who had fought with William at the Boyne but was now out of favour. Another was John, Earl of Mar and titular duke, a man who changed sides so often that he was nicknamed 'Bobbing John'. These two were instrumental in fomenting riots in the West Country, to the point that the Riot Act was passed giving magistrates the arbitrary power to use violence to quell provincial unrest.

Meanwhile James was continuing with his little court and dealing entirely with the trivia of designing commissions and titles for the 'busy flies that all day buzz about me', although he did make the sensible appointment of Bolingbroke as secretary of state. However, when Ormonde fled to France in August, the Jacobite support in the west of England collapsed, and Mar, rashly and unbidden, raised the standard of revolution at Perth on 6 September 1715, arranging for vessels to be available in four Channel ports for James's conveyance to a triumphant return. Bolingbroke prepared a manifesto for James which the king edited down to a simple declaration of Catholic bigotry.

Thanks to superior intelligence, the London Government was aware of all Jacobite moves, and Ormonde's futile attempts to land on the Devon coast were easily repulsed. Unco-ordinated skirmishes were equally easily crushed, and the only real threat came from the opportunistic Mar who advanced towards Dunblane, joining battle at Sheriffmuir on 13 November. The battle was indecisive but Mar retreated to Perth where he was, at last, joined by a reluctant James in late December 1715. James was naturally withdrawn and aloof, disliking close contact with strangers, and his haughty tone and lack of charisma failed to inspire the clansmen, unlike his son who would achieve this so effectively 30 years later. By 4 February 1716 James realised that he had no chance of victory, so with Mar he sailed back to France.

His Highland supporters had found James 'heavy going' and he was probably suffering from one of his frequent attacks of stress-borne collapse. James did not lack courage, but given a choice between fight or flight he would allow events to overtake him and then flee.

But Louis XIV was now dead, and the regent Orléans made it clear that James could no longer enjoy the latitude he had been allowed by the old regime. Having passed through France he retired to what would now be his permanent home at the Palazzo Muti. He dismissed Bolingbroke and set about solving more immediate problems than restoration. The 1715 rising had hardly been more than a display of overweening ambition by others which he had been forced to join.

James's immediate problems were twofold. He had no reliable income apart from occasional grants from the Vatican, and these depended entirely on the personal whim of Clement XI. Second, he needed an heir. The solution to both of these problems would be found in a rich marriage.

As always he chose the path of least resistance and approached his grandfather the Duke of Modena, whose daughter Benedicta was personally rich and carried suitable titles of nobility. Also, although he had never seen Benedicta, he may have hoped that she might remind him of Mary of Modena, his mother, who would die two years later. The fact that such a union was well within the bounds of the ban on marriage between close relatives and would need a very special dispensation by the pope seemed not to worry James. As it turned out, neither he nor Benedicta need have worried. Perhaps James's reputation as a gloomily inert pessimist had reached the Duke, or perhaps he felt that one union with a Stuart, one that had led to exile and disgrace, was enough. Therefore James's suit was peremptorily turned down.

James's policy was that if at first you don't succeed, then give up, and he passed the responsibility for the search to one Charles Wogan of Rathcoffey, an Irish aristocrat who had been an officer in the 1715 rising and was already a trusted ambassador who could be relied on to be an effective wooer. Wogan was indeed 'such a wooer, gay, witty, brave and handsome'. This dashing cavalier visited the courts of Westphalia and Bavaria searching for rich Catholic heiresses, and in Ohlau, Silesia – present-day Poland – he met Princess Maria Clementina Sobieska.

Her lineage was impeccable since her grandfather was Jan Sobieski, who had led the Christian army which had saved Vienna from the Turks in 1683. She was the youngest daughter of Prince James Sobieski and was reputedly beautiful, small and high-spirited, 'gay only in season', although these attributes were of little consequence to James. A cloud no bigger than a man's hand was that her father was a depressive and her mother notably unstable. Clementina herself was occasionally morbidly pious, but these incipient disadvantages were ignored.

The wedding was delayed when Clementina was arrested en route for Rome at the behest of George I, but after a six-month imprisonment at Ohlau in Silesia she was rescued by the gallant Wogan in a 'Quixotade' and arrived in Bologna to find that her prospective husband had gone to Spain.

He was hoping to take part in a Jacobite rising under the auspices of Cardinal Alberoni, but the fleet got no further than Corunna when it was wrecked in a storm. Co-ordination of intelligence was not a strong point of the Jacobites, and this news did not reach George Keith, the Earl Marischal, who had landed with some Spanish troops at Stornoway on the Isle of Lewis. Since Alberoni's force did not appear, Keith sailed with his tiny force for the mainland and on 9 June 1719 reached Glenshiel, where they were easily routed. This rising had been so disregarded by London that there were no punishments and the rebels were quietly allowed to disperse.

Back in Italy and lacking a husband, Clementina went through a marriage ceremony, with James Murray acting as a proxy for James, on 9 May, and the real wedding took place on 2 September 1719. James was impressed by the appearance of his bride, but Clementina was disappointed in her husband. Wogan had been romantic and adventurous as well as handsome, but James was dour, tired from a fruitless journey across Europe and more than usually uncharismatic.

However, Pope Clement XI gave the couple a country estate at Albano as a summer residence and by the summer of 1720 Clementina was declared pregnant. The Stuart dynasty could now continue and the child, born on 31 December, was christened Charles Edward Louis Casimir Silvester Severino Maria Stuart. His multiplicity of forenames showed James's wish to stress his friendship with the great houses of Europe, from which he received letters of congratulation, although only the pope sent money – the paltry sum of 10,000 scudi.

In England the South Sea Bubble was about to burst, bringing discredit on the Whig system of rampant capitalism. The time was right for a restoration attempt, but James did nothing except to bicker with his wife over the choice of nurses for his new prince.

A Jacobite plot in England was, however, uncovered in 1722, again involving Bishop Atterbury. The royal family was to be kidnapped and James III proclaimed king. The plot was exposed and all those involved were arrested. One man, Layer, was hanged, drawn and quartered, while Atterbury was sentenced to perpetual exile. James made no attempt to give any support to the plotters.

A younger brother to Charles Edward was born in March 1725 and christened Henry Benedict by the incoming Pope Benedict XIII. The marital distance between the royal couple increased as they differed over the education of their sons. There were now two almost separate courts, with Clementina vigorously ensuring that Henry was steeped in the Catholic faith. James, for his part, concentrated on turning the young Prince Charles into a model of eighteenth-century manhood, to the horror of his wife. She asserted that her husband wished to bring the boys up as heretics, and rather than permit such an infamy she would stab them with her own hand. Thus Charles grew up in a maelstrom of family discord. He excelled at riding, shooting and fencing. He was even allowed to attend a siege as part of a limited military education. Admired for his skill and grace on the dance floor, he continued to grow tall and fair-headedly handsome with witty and gracious charm. He was also proficient in playing the cello, an activity which he maintained to the end of his life. His spelling was at best idiosyncratic and he could speak Italian, English and French, all of them imperfectly, while his brother, thanks to his mother's influence, easily outperformed him in Latin.

James took no care to educate Charles Edward in politics or diplomacy, and there was no sign that he was being raised as a Crown Prince to inherit a throne from a restored father. When he was 13, he took a violent dislike to Lord Dunbar as a governor, and had to be confined to his room with all weapons placed out of reach. This was the first sign of an inherent violent temper which burst out when he was corrected.

The royal couple were now virtually living apart, James at Albano and Clementina in Rome, where she would enter a convent in 1727. Charles had, in the normal sense, lost his mother, for reasons he had no chance of understanding, at the age of six and a half. They met occasionally with a certain formality. Charles once wrote to his father, 'I will be very dutiful to Mamma, and not jump too near her.' In the convent Clementina declined into the religious mania which had beset her mother, undertaking horrifying fasts and mortification of the flesh. She died eight years later, in 1735. Charles was 15 years old.

Marriage for either of the princes was a possibility, but there were only half-hearted attempts to find a wealthy noble bride for Charles. Such a marriage would have eased James's reliance on papal handouts, but in 1737 he became one of the wealthiest men in Europe. Clementina's father, James Sobieski, died and James inherited the family wealth, including the famous Sobieski jewels. Cynics have argued that gaining this inheritance had been his sole reason for marrying Clementina, and given his treatment of her after she had provided the required 'heir and a spare' their arguments have some merit.

Both Clementina's personal jewellery and the crown jewels of Poland now belonged to James, and he placed them on deposit with the Monte di Pietà in Rome. This was a kind of national pawn shop on a grand scale and the security solved the problem of Stuart liquidity. Apart from short vacations James never left Rome again.

This new-found freedom caused no activity in James and he continued in his accustomed lethargy, thus in many ways depriving Charles Edward of a father figure, a lack he would feel at crucial moments in his later life. There was no one in his early life who would serve as a model and so he would have to invent himself.

As for James, he was content to be James III – after all, Louis XIV had declared him so – and to be a king in exile. He had seen his father lead the rising in Ireland, albeit to a defeat. He had arrived in Scotland as the 1715 rising had exhausted itself and had returned immediately to Rome, having been no more than a visitor. His journey to Spain in 1719 was made in time to receive the news that the fleet had already sailed and sunk. The cross-Europe journey also coincided with his missing his own wedding. He corresponded with the high Tory Atterbury and gave verbal support to his Jacobitism but no concrete encouragement. The Jacobite exiles in Europe had all found profitable niches in other regimes and had no wish to uproot themselves again. Possibly, if Charles Edward had been successful in 1745, James, under pressure, would have travelled to London and taken the crown; but he would have had to be offered the crown first, setting in motion the repeal of the Act of Settlement, and he certainly showed no sign of ambition to bring about a Stuart restoration. That idea would belong to his elder son.

Chapter 3

The clan chiefs gave their support to Charles Edward out of loyalty to the Stuarts and often against their own interests

It has often been said that Scottish kings ruled only with the consent of the nobility, and in 1745 many of the nobility felt no sympathy at all for the Hanoverian kings in London and a positive hatred for the Act of Union of 1707, which had seen parliamentary power shift to London. Resentment against England had also increased in the central midlands and south of Scotland with the failure of the Darien Scheme. This had been a lunatic enterprise in 1698 to colonise the uninhabitable region of Darien, or Panama. It would, at a stroke, have damaged England's trading interests in the region and antagonised Spain. A total lack of information over local conditions resulted in attempts to trade wigs and woollen cloth with a native population that endured some of the highest temperatures and levels of humidity on the planet, and the spectacular failure of the scheme brought

Scotland to the brink of bankruptcy. Part of the Act of Union provided for the Equivalent, a cash payment of £400,000 to compensate for Scotland's massive losses in the Darien Scheme, and there was strong feeling that London had dragged its feet in payment, or that the subsidy had gone, as subsidies will, into the wrong hands.

The emotional independence of the Highlander had been further eroded by the Disarming Acts of 1715 and 1725 which forbade the carrying of arms in public. Daggers of varying lengths were carried as 'hunting knives', and the universally thatched roofs made excellent hiding places for broadswords and axes, ensuring ease of rapid retrieval when opportunities arose. Lord Lovat, a Highland noble who claimed that his family was Norman French – with 'fraise' being corrupted to 'Fraser' – had dubious loyalties and a seat at Westminster. He obliged the Government by informing them on the state of the Highlands. He claimed that blackmail, by which he meant the racket of enforced protection, was widespread, that only Hanoverian supporters had yielded up their arms, and also that Jacobites were now being appointed to positions of high office.

London's response was the building of forts at key spots in the Highlands, and General Wade was appointed as a commander-in-chief of government forces in 1725. To some this looked like military occupation by a foreign power. To alleviate these fears a watch regiment with local knowledge was formed to police the Highlands, and this would form the basis of the regiment of the Black Watch.

Scotland was still an agrarian nation with little to export apart from livestock and linen, and the waves of prosperity experienced by the often newly ennobled Whig oligarchies in the south seldom washed up north of the border and were even more rarely seen by the old Tory aristocracy of the Highlands.

The origins of the names 'Whig' and 'Tory' are doubtful, obscure and best ignored. Suffice it to say that the Hanoverians were Whig to the core. Their power base was one rooted in trade and commerce, although the philosopher and historian David Hume would have said that Whigs believed in 'Parliament and Protestantism' while Tories followed 'Catholicism and the Crown' – in this case the exiled crown of the Stuarts. He also felt that Whiggery was more democratic, although in the Georgian period their supporters cheerfully ignored the fact that their wealth and subsequent power often came from corruption and trade gained after sometimes brutal conquest. The Tory wealth, on the other hand, was derived from the land, either by agriculture or by the multiplicity of tenures.

Nowhere was this difference between land-based wealth and trade-based prosperity seen more acutely than in Scotland, where in the Highlands the wealth lay entirely in the produce of the land in the sway of the great nobles, divided up in a feudal system dating back hundreds of years. The clan system – *clann* in Scottish Gaelic simply meant 'children' – was defined by a unity of people of the same surname inevitably living in close communities. They worked the land by agreement of their chiefs, who were entitled to wear an eagle's feather in their bonnets and often did, although some of them actually owned very little land but could, traditionally, rely on a large proportion of what that land produced. It was divided into smaller and smaller plots, until at the bottom of the heap was the 'tacksman'. He was the feudal subject of his 'chief' who allowed him to farm on his land in return for being able to claim a large proportion of the crops or livestock. The tacksman could not move from the land and his life was entirely at the laird's disposal. He was allowed to sell any surplus, but money played little part in his life, which was largely that of a subsistence farmer, usually on poor soil, eked out with eggs, milk and occasionally fish.

This system had already started to crumble as chiefs realised that they could make more economic use of their land-holdings. Many were educated in the south, some in England, were often well travelled, multi-lingual and used to the luxuries of eighteenth-century gentlemen. A new system would free the tacksmen, who would raise cash crops from which they would earn money to pay rent. The chiefs' wealth would come not from the extent of what was owned, and what could be produced from it, but from what it could be made to earn in terms of rent. A capitalist cash economy was replacing what had been a feudal system in all but name. The Argyll Campbells, for instance, were freeing their tacksmen and leasing smallholdings to them for cash. The smallholders, equivalent to today's crofter, would pay rent to the laird, raised by whatever means they could. But they were freemen. The laird could, of course, terminate their agreements at any time and the smallholders were still subject to his goodwill in all things. This was the agrarian capitalism of the Whigs replacing the feudal clan system of the Tories.

When Charles landed in 1745, first on Eriskay and then at Moidart, he sent out a call for these clan chieftains to rally to his cause. The majority of the chiefs did not wish to destroy anything or even to turn the clock back. But they did want to stop the clock. As far as they could see, this new capitalism was in the hands of the Whigs and had been given to London by the Act of Union in 1707. A Scottish king ruling an independent Scotland from Edinburgh would suit them very well, and Charles Edward seemed to be the man to bring a focus to their desires.

However, as always in history, the story was much more complicated. The Scottish clan system made sense in a sparsely populated land with poor communications. At least it did until General Wade started to construct a network of roads. For centuries, under the 'regelian rights', the Highland chiefs had enjoyed the power of 'pit and gallows' unimpeded by any legislation from Edinburgh or, even worse, from London. It seemed to many that the Whigs were bent on removing their hereditary powers. Charles Edward seemed to represent a bulwark against this and when his call went out they were curious to hear his proposals.

There was no demand for a *levée en masse* since that would have required unanimity among the clans, many of whom had been enemies for generations. Also many of the clan chiefs were converted to the Whig cause. The massive Campbell clan, the Monroes of Ross, the Sutherland Mackays and in Caithness the Sinclairs and Dunbars remained aloof from the rising. Some clan chiefs, however, regarded a request from the man they saw as their king as an absolute command. All they knew was that Charles Edward was the true son of the man whose grandfather had been the last King of Scotland and that he was to raise an army to restore his father to his rightful place. Whether that place was London or Edinburgh and whether the Union of Scotland and England would survive were questions best left unanswered for the moment.

Charles's first rejection by the Skye clan chiefs on Eriskay was a shock to a man used to universal agreement to his plans, but their reasons for refusal were valid. He had promised them that he would land with 6,000 French troops to support his cause. Louis must 'take off the mask, or have eternal shame'. In reality, there were no French troops. Also, much of Charles's artillery and siege equipment had been on his supply ship the *Elizabeth*, which had been forced to limp away after an encounter with the Royal Navy.

To the Skye chiefs the Stuart cause seemed lost before the Prince had even landed on the mainland, and it demonstrates a crucial point.

In any conflict the normal wish of any participant is to be on the winning side, and it seemed as if the Jacobites were already the losing side, with its supporters liable to the inevitable punishment and revenge when Charles was predictably defeated.

The choices facing the clan chiefs were complex. They could come out openly for the status quo and support the Hanoverian side. If it prevailed they would be no worse off, and they might even see some liberality from London, although their land-holdings were so remote that this was unlikely. If they supported the Jacobites and Charles won they might expect royal favour, but if he lost they would expect punishment of some sort, and without French support he looked like a loser. To do nothing would simply give them the excuse that they were too poor to get involved.

For Charles the dilemma was what would happen if their lack of confidence spread to other clans. Boisdale had said that he would warn other MacDonald clans including the Clanranalds, a devout Catholic clan. Charles, with his usual impetuosity, moved at once to stem the damage and sailed for Moidart, where he issued a rallying call to the clans. Since, technically, they were all his tacksmen this would be more difficult to ignore.

But without a mass rising there had to be a unity of purpose among the rebels, with Charles and the clansmen united in a common purpose. And as events would prove, this was sadly lacking.

Nothing daunted, Charles ordered the unshipment of what munitions he still had and dismissed the *Doutelle*, a French ship that was his last link with outside help. Then he managed to persuade young Ranald MacDonald to join him. This showed a political shrewdness which his father lacked, since by the codes of honour Clanranald had to support a kinsman, and he swore the support of his clan. Glencoe and Keppoch followed their leader and Charles could claim that he was assembling an army.

The ambivalence of the clan chiefs is best shown by the attitude of Cameron of Lochiel. Charles wrote to Lochiel, who replied by sending his brother with advice for Charles to return to France. The next step in this medieval dance of protocol was for Charles to demand a face-to-face meeting. Lochiel started the discussion by, quite reasonably, asking where Charles's promised French troops were. Charles said that the French would augment a Jacobite army when it was already in the field, adding that his army would be led by the

Earl Marischal and would proceed no matter what Lochiel decided.

This put Lochiel on his chivalric mettle and he now set out his terms. First was the demand that in the event of the rising's failure Charles would guarantee him no financial or territorial losses. The Prince, with the Sobieski wealth in mind, agreed, although in fact his war chest held only £4,000.

Lochiel then asked if the chief of the Glengarry MacDonalds would give a written assurance of support. Charles told him that such an undertaking had been made, and Lochiel then pledged his clansmen's loyalty. He now had assurances that his personal wealth and status were safe and there would be a viable fighting force. His personal interests and those of Clan Cameron were now protected.

His feudal loyalty had stretched as far as meeting his prince and hearing what he had had to say. Then he made very sure that he did not act against his own interests or those of his clan, and he knew very well that the initial success of the rising depended on his participation. He could therefore demand terms which would be beyond lesser clans. The idea that Charles might be lying never seemed to enter his aristocratic mind and Charles could now proceed to Glenfinnan for the raising of his standard.

He was joined by some northern lairds – the clan system did not operate in the North-East, although the system of tacksmen did – one of whom, John Gordon of Glenbucket, already had a Hanoverian prisoner in the form of Colonel Swithenham, whom he had captured as he attempted to join the garrison at Fort William. The Jacobite forces were now swollen by the Clanranald men as well as 300 Keppochs and

700 Camerons – who had followed Lochiel only after he threatened to burn their belongings and cottages. This was not in any way a spontaneous rising.

Charles, for all his Stuart grandeur, always managed a common touch, and his charm could make allies among the most unlikely people. But now he was deprived of this skill, since he spoke Italian, French and English, even though his grasp of these was always uneven, but no Gaelic, the language of north-western Scotland. The chiefs spoke Gaelic, English, and often French and Latin, and Charles had to use them as his translators. Direct communication with his forces was all but impossible. But the feudal bond between Prince and chief was strong, when it was to the chief's advantage.

The rising now had an impetus of its own and Charles marched south with increased confidence. His arrival and march had been noted by James Mor Macgregor, a son of Rob Roy and like his father a government spy, and had been duly reported to Edinburgh. Charles's confidence paid off as he was joined by the Stewarts of Appin, and 500 men from the Glengarry MacDonalds, from both Keppoch and Glencoe, swelled his ranks. The news that the Hanoverian General Sir John Cope had dashed to Inverness rather than face the Jacobites enhanced their reputation, and further recruits joined the Prince's army. It should be noted that Cope had been defeated by Marshal Saxe at Fontenay in the Netherlands on 11 May, and his army was demoralised and exhausted. By 4 September Charles was in Perth where he declared his father James III as King of Great Britain.

Undoubtedly Charles's most important recruit was Lord George Murray, a 59-year-old veteran of previous campaigns, eminently suited to fill the position of father figure which Charles had been lacking almost from birth. Winchester-educated, Murray was suspected of lack of loyalty by many of Charles's closest companions, since he had until a fortnight earlier served under General Cope, but Charles ignored this and immediately appointed him as Lieutenant-General of his army.

But it was no ordinary army. Recruitment had often been enforced by lairds or clan chiefs hoping to profit from the overthrow of the London Whigs, and was seldom inspired by simple zealotry for the Stuart cause. Bands of followers would desert if they felt that they were not profiting from the advance, or when their own harvests needed to be taken in. Often clan chiefs would not attend in person but send deputies. Roderick Chisholm of Strathglass, for example, sent his fifth son with only four or five clansmen.

Thanks to the loss of the supply ship the *Elizabeth* the army was ill-equipped and had to seize arms and equipment as they advanced. This meant that the clansmen were frequently unpaid and ill-fed, resulting in outbreaks of looting. This was something Charles abhorred and he took strong, if ineffectual, action to prevent it.

Murray also had problems in keeping the clansmen united, since for generations most clans had been the mortal enemies of their neighbours, stealing each other's sheep and cattle, to say nothing of women. They were experts at the midnight raid, ambush and surprise, but disciplined campaigning was a new concept and they often complained at the speed of Charles's march. He took great pleasure in indulging in physical exercise and marched briskly ahead of his forces.

The novelty of sleeping like his men, wrapped only in a plaid, exhilarated him although he did take advantage of more comfortable quarters when they were available.

By 17 September 1745 the Jacobite army had reached Coltbridge on the western outskirts of Edinburgh, and the city's citizens held their collective breath. Since they knew almost nothing of Highlanders they were expecting rape and pillage by savage barbarians on a grand scale. What little they did know stemmed only from acquaintance with sedan-chair carriers in the city – burly giants from the glens speaking Gaelic, a language totally foreign to the city dwellers – and rumours of the most outlandish sort flourished. There was a contemporary cartoon of two Highlanders gazing in puzzled wonderment at a lavatory and debating its possible use.

The Edinburgh-based author David Hume expressed a popular opinion when he said:

The Highlanders are as ignorant of Discipline as are the Low Country Ploughmen and know as little the Nature of Encampments, Marches, Ranks, Evolutions … The barbarous Highlander, living chiefly by pasturage has leisure to cultivate the idea of military honour … he soon fancies that he himself was born a hero as well as a gentleman.

Alexander Carlyle met two Highlanders who when he gave them a shilling went off happy, and a Jacobite officer told him that the army would desert en masse when they had full bellies. The citizens' fears were unfounded, but Hume and Carlyle had one thing in common. They were dyed-in-the-wool Whigs, and the Highland leaders were, principally, the product of generations of Tories. The difference was absolute and was at one of the roots of the failure of the '45.

Unity of purpose is paramount in such a venture and the only purpose which united the clans was the desperate hope that they would improve their conditions, by the restoration of James either as King of Great Britain – Charles's declared purpose – or as King of Scotland. Charles provided a focus and a leadership which had hitherto been absent, except possibly from the Duke of Argyll, now on the Hanoverian side. No one wanted to jeopardise their own interests. But they were reasonably happy, if given sufficient security, to follow a leader who might free them from the Hanoverian yoke, while still having doubts as to his personal ambition for himself. Regent or King?

Chapter 4

He rejected the idea of an independent Scotland and marched into England to become King of Great Britain

This is almost certainly true, but to discover Charles's personal ambitions we must examine his childhood, where by force of circumstances he had to invent himself. After a birthing that included five full days of labour for Clementina, with almost 100 lookers-on, Charles was born as the prince of an exiled king. His father had been an exile for 38 years and had no real hope of regaining his kingdom. He had managed to marry a rich heiress although he lived mainly on the charity of Pope Clement XI, who sent him 10,000 scudi as a present to celebrate the birth, and Charles was christened into the Catholic faith by Bishop Bonaventura. His immediate prospects were to be a phantom prince living on the charity of others.

There were, at first, worries about the Prince's health, but after a change of nurse, and by the time he was four years old, his health had improved and a tutor had to be found. He already spoke some English, although badly, and his Italian and French were 'very little worse'. He would go on to learn Latin, although he spoke none of these languages perfectly. By this time he was 'lusty and running about', and the choice of education was a problem for James.

Should he educate the boy to one day take the throne of Britain? Or train him as a dilettante prince to spend his life in European exile? James did what he did best and tried to ignore the problem by hiring a tutor who was guaranteed to exacerbate the dilemma. He was Michael Ramsay, the self-styled 'Chevalier' Ramsay. He was what today would be called a 'chancer', the son of an Ayrshire baker who had been a student of Fenelon's at Cambrai, who was created a knight of the somewhat doubtful Order of St Lazarus and had tactfully dedicated a book to James. He had been living in Paris as part of the Jacobite faction allied to the Earl of Mar since the '15, and he started his work in the Palazzo Muti in January 1724 with a vague educational theory of developing character rather than learning by specific subject. His philosophy of passive acceptance, learned from Fenelon, neatly coincided with James's inactivity and habitual vacillation, but after only nine months Atterbury exposed Mar as a turncoat, and James felt that Ramsay may have been infected. Washing his hands of the affair, James gave Ramsay a colonelcy and sent him packing in November of the same year.

James was devoted to his son, whom he had created a Knight of the Garter in 1722, and decided that he should henceforth be cared for by men, thus antagonising his wife and causing a conflict of loyalties for the Prince. James Murray, now created Earl of Dunbar, was put in place as Charles's governor, with Thomas Sheridan as an under-governor.

Sheridan was a Catholic while Dunbar was, inconveniently, a confirmed Protestant. Thus James had, with his usual political ineptitude, muddied the waters and sown confusion in his son's psyche. This move, unsurprisingly, drove Clementina into a blind fury and she took refuge in an Ursuline convent, plunging deeper and deeper into religious mania. The marital row became the gossip of Europe, diminishing the already dwindling Jacobite support.

In March 1725 Clementina had given birth to Henry Benedict, and from this time Charles's sense of isolation increased, especially when his mother poured poison into Pope Benedict XIII's ear with the false rumour that James intended to raise Charles as a Protestant. The result was that Benedict instructed the Inquisition to keep a watch on the Palazzo Muti. In response to this the ever-suspicious James gave instruction that Charles should be seized on his morning ride and then confined to the palace. There were further rumours that the Prince was turning against the Church, even being reputed to say that the Mass had cost his grandfather three kingdoms.

James attempted to solve the problem of separation by moving his entire court to Bologna, leaving Clementina in Rome. Bologna was a papal state and the newly elected Benedict XIII would not allow Charles to live there under the tutelage of Dunbar, a Protestant, until he had reassured himself as to the child's devotion to the Catholic faith. Therefore the six-year-old was summoned to the papal presence, and having petulantly refused to kiss the papal feet, as protocol required, was subjected to a one-to-one interrogation on the Catholic faith after reciting selected chunks of the catechism. This did nothing to reduce Charles's already massive state of insecurity.

Physically the boy was flourishing, and even allowing for the sycophancy surrounding such opinions he was admired as a naturally gifted horseman. At the age of six he attended his first ball, displaying his increasing prowess as a dancer. He was being educated in fencing and shooting with cross-bows with which he was an accomplished marksman. Still too young to be educated in politics or history, subjects essential for a future heir to a throne, he was excelling in the 'manly arts' as well as displaying a pleasant turn of wit.

The conflict between James and Clementina cooled down and in 1727 she travelled to Bologna to be reunited with her husband. Charles was to have both parents with him again, having been motherless for the best part of two years. But on 10 June 1727 George I died on his way to Osnabrück, and James left in a half-hearted attempt to reach England and raise Jacobite support in northern Europe, leaving Charles fatherless for six months.

James's trip was fruitless since France forbade him from crossing her territories, and he ended up in Avignon, still a papal fief. Back in Rome Clementina began a regime of fasting and mortification of the flesh. James returned to his now deranged wife and, seizing Charles, set out on a tour of northern Italy. This was a chance to show off his son and Charles duly shone in society, charming ladies and delighting noblemen with his wit. He also took up golf at which he became expert.

By April 1729 father and son were back at the Palazzo Muti and Charles's relationship with his mother was mainly carried on by letter while he socialised in Rome under the watchful eye of his melancholic father. There were feeble enquiries into possible marriages and a futile proposal that Charles should continue his education abroad, possibly in France, which was unfortunately bound by treaty with England not to aid the Stuarts. Switzerland was considered, but thought to be too Protestant. Domestically Charles was outstripped academically by his younger brother, and could not enjoy any kind of childhood while being shipped from one warring parent to the other and living nomadically with his not altogether sympathetic governors. In September 1733 Charles had a furious row with Dunbar, kicking him and threatening to murder him if he dared to chastise him. Charles was locked in his room until James felt he had learned his lesson.

The year 1734 was decisive in Charles's education since Spanish armies were besieging Gaeta, on the road to Naples, and Charles was invited to join them. After some procrastination by James, arrangements were made and Charles, aged 14 and supposedly travelling incognito simply as 'the Young Chevalier de St George', visited the army with five coach-loads of servants. He was allowed to watch a bombardment from a safe distance, and went to visit the trenches, albeit during the siesta hours, where mounted on a little horse he astonished everyone by addressing the soldiers in their own languages. His charm was equally evident when attending the balls and receptions arranged for him, and although only a young teenager he started to realise that he was very capable of organising his life away from the dark intrigues of the Palazzo Muti.

James was angry at Charles's new popularity. But Charles's bid for freedom with the army was cut short by his mother's death in January 1735 and he was forced to return to Rome.

As far as a Stuart restoration was concerned James wanted to wait until the time was ripe, and he was a man for whom the time would never be ripe. The 1737 mission of John Gordon of Glenbucket, bringing news of growing Jacobite strength in Scotland, did nothing to enliven his spirits.

Events beyond his control in the autumn of 1743 forced his hand. Louis XV sent spies to England to investigate Jacobite feeling, and it became known that Charles's presence in France would be welcome, although he would have to remain incognito to avoid rousing English suspicions. Thus at 3 a.m. on 8 January 1744 Charles and his father had an hour-long private conversation, after which Charles left Rome in disguise. Thus James bade farewell to his 'Carluccio', his pet name for his son. The two men would never meet again.

Letters granting Charles powers of regency had been prepared, but whether the Prince was carrying them is unknown. At any rate, after a journey of disguises and deceptions he was in Paris by 8 February. Diplomatically, his incognito was maintained, but when attending the opera Charles wore a mask but also the star and sash of the Order of the Garter, raising his mask to acknowledge the cheers of the crowd. Anonymity was not a favourite role for Charles Edward.

The initial idea was that the French would send an army under Marshal Saxe to invade the south coast of England while the English Jacobites rose in support. Charles waited at Gravelines to cross the Channel and claim his father's throne. But severe storms – 'Protestant winds' – and a complete lack of secrecy allowed the English to fortify the Channel and the attempt had to be called off.

Charles had been in contact with the Highland chiefs, and a landing in Scotland was proposed while the French would land simultaneously in England. Charles had been using Lord Sempill as an ambassador to Louis XV and on 15 March he wrote to Sempill begging him to get Louis to allow Charles to leave France. Louis prevaricated and eventually the French landing was postponed until after Charles had assembled his Highland army. On 22 June, frustrated at his continued 'French imprisonment', he set sail from the Loire estuary on board the *Doutelle,* a 16-gun frigate, meeting up with the 64-gun man o' war *Elizabeth* which carried 700 Irish Jacobites and the arms, ammunition, field guns and siege equipment needed for a serious campaign. On 20 March they were spotted by the *Lion*, an English warship, and the resulting engagement left the *Elizabeth* limping back to port in France. The *Doutelle* made it to Eriskay but the military matériel was lost.

Charles landed on the tiny island and in August he sailed to Moidart and Glenfinnan, where the '45 was launched.

On Tuesday 17 September 1745 he entered Edinburgh and immediately held a triumphal parade at the foot of Arthur's Seat. In the brief time of his success he became addicted to triumphal parades. He is described as being five feet ten inches tall with light brown hair turning gold at the tips, covered by a pale periwig. He wore a tartan short coat and the order of St Andrew. This was echoed by the cockade in his bonnet, being of a white saltire cross, and for the first time someone referred to him as 'Bonnie Prince Charlie'.

As soon as Charles was established in the city, the heralds and pursuivants, splendid in their tabards, met at the Mercat

Cross and declared James III as rightful king with Prince Charles as his regent.

His victory was not complete, since General Cope was still encamped to the east of Edinburgh, and on 21 September the Jacobites surprised the Hanoverian forces under General John Cope at Prestonpans in a daring dawn attack. Before the attack Charles drew his sword and announced that he had thrown away his scabbard. 'Mr Cope shall not escape us.' The dawn assault was a total success, with an estimated 1,500 prisoners taken and Charles stopping the inevitable slaughter since 'the men are my father's subjects'. He was keen to emphasise his position as no more than a regent.

Scotland was now Jacobite territory. Charles held court at the palace of Holyrood, choosing to ignore the fact that the castle, which dominated the city, had not yet surrendered. He now had to consider his next move and faced two options. First, he could assemble his Highlanders and under Lord George Murray march south to London. Second, he could summon a parliament and use it to secede from the 38-year-old Act of Union and declare his father King of Scotland. He could do this with every hope that his father would never leave the Palazzo Muti and that he would endorse Charles as regent until the time when his death would bring the crown to Charles.

The clan chiefs and lairds – Catholics, Episcopalians or Tories – would be delighted to a man to be ruled by a King of Scotland in Edinburgh, and their tenants and tacksmen would follow where they were led. The commercial power in Scotland was centred on Edinburgh, and the merchants were mainly Whig, but Whig with no love for London, a town described by one local man as 'inhabited by barbarians living on the banks of the Thames'.

The clergy had feared a Catholic domination, but Charles insisted that the Protestant churches remain open, although only the minister of the West Kirk obeyed. Society had flocked to Charles's court at Holyrood, and his programmes of balls and parties had endeared himself to them. Personally he could have had no reason to move on.

Militarily he was on less secure ground. Although there was now no Hanoverian army in Scotland, he had only about 2,300 men under arms. He had taken 1,500 prisoners at Prestonpans, many of whom would now join him, in spite of having sworn not to do so when they had enlisted under Cope. He had sent Jacobite surgeons to treat the wounded and had thus enhanced his reputation for mercy among the population.

Charles summoned a Grand Council to debate his next move but the council quickly formed two groups. One was headed by Charles and the other by the older person of Lord George Murray, who apart from being commander-in-chief became the father figure the 24-year-old Charles had always lacked. Lord George's first move was to send an envoy to England to investigate and mobilise the English Jacobites. The envoy crossed the border into Northumberland and was immediately arrested.

The council was split, with Charles advocating an immediate continuation of his successful impetus with the invasion of England. Murray pointed out that they had too few forces, given that they could expect desertions to increase as they advanced further into England. He had history on his side, in that all Scottish incursions into England had been failures. Charles's education had ignored these uncomfortable facts. His reinforcements in Edinburgh had been few, and a letter from Lady Mackintosh of Moy gives us a snapshot of conditions. Her spelling is even worse than the Prince's:

> The bearer of this has a company Ressed for the Prince's service but was hindered by Lord Siforth to keray them off, which meks me geve this trouble to beg of your grace to give hem an order for resting his men. And thene he can wouse a little force.

Lady Mackintosh, soon to be nicknamed 'Colonel Anne', had plenty of loyalty, but her support in a formal eighteenth-century campaign was minimal. The Scots were experts at raids into England and mounting quick border incursions, but lengthy campaigns had never succeeded since the days of the Pictish raids on the Roman province. In spite of Charles's interdictions there would be looting, and the further south the army advanced the further the loot had to be carried. They would also travel further and further from reliable sources of food, and the Jacobite commissary was ill-stocked and in an even worse state of organisation. It was also extremely dangerous to leave the forts and castles in Government hands, and Charles, having lost his siege equipment with the loss of the *Elizabeth*, had no way of capturing them.

Stay in Edinburgh, restore the Stuart monarchy in a once more independent Scotland, build up your forces and war chest, and consider the future calmly. This was the advice of Lord George Murray. Advocating calm reflection to Charles

Edward Stuart was like suggesting to a starving man, at last seated at the table, that he should wait a few more hours for the gourmet menu.

But Charles was dealt a trump card to play by the arrival at Montrose of the Marquis d'Eguilles, a special envoy from Louis XV. It seemed that what Charles had always promised, French reinforcements, was coming to fruition, and Murray could no longer counsel delay. It was, however, a false dawn.

Events in Europe had been forcing action. Pope Benedict was so delighted at Charles's success that he sent further finance to Charles's brother Henry while pressing Louis XV to take action. Louis was also under pressure from the various Jacobite factions in France. But Louis hated pressure nearly as much as he hated taking any kind of action. Thus he did what he did best. He delayed while seeming to respond, sending d'Eguilles on a fact-finding mission. But d'Eguilles also brought siege equipment, engineers and artillery, arriving in time to receive the cheering news of Prestonpans.

The result of this was that France signed the Treaty of Fontainebleau, allying herself to the Jacobite cause. But since Louis was not willing to commit ground forces, all this did was to muddy the already dark waters.

Matters in Edinburgh came to a head with the council meeting on 30 October. Lord George asserted that the Jacobites were undermanned and liable to lose more men as winter approached. Better to let the clans return to the glens and build up their strength for a spring offensive. Charles, however, knew that he could only keep his army together by giving it constant activity and continual progress. He argued strongly that their numbers would swell with English

Jacobites, but Lord George doubted this and gave chilling estimates of what Government forces awaited them across the border. The older, experienced soldier was appalled by Charles's opportunistic plans, but still flushed with the success at Prestonpans Charles urged an immediate advance into Northumberland to engage Cope before the general had time to organise his admittedly superior forces.

Charles allowed Lord George a minor victory, and on 31 October the Jacobite army set out, not for Newcastle but for Carlisle. They carried with them the conflicting principles of caution and opportunity, of tried and trusted theory at war with as yet untested adventure and daring. They also left behind them any hope of an independent Scotland under a Stuart dynasty. Charles's target was London.

In fact it had been London from the start, although Charles had been careful not to be so explicit to the chiefs and lairds supporting him. Neither he nor his father had ever visited London in any real sense, although James had been born there before being spirited out of the country at the age of three. He would have been aware of the warming-pan slander, but his youth had been the peripatetic life of an exile, with London no more than a golden memory.

For Charles too, it represented a dream of being in real power, no longer dependent on the charity of popes or French kings and with a household which also represented the nearest version of a loving family that a prince could hope for. He knew it only in the much-polished legends of other dispossessed exiles, and its total repossession was his breathing ambition as well as his duty. He had no interest whatsoever in Scotland or its crown, and his father had only visited the country at the end of an unsuccessful rising 30 years previously. His experience of Scotsmen was tainted by the behaviour of the Earl of Mar and the attitudes of the clan chiefs, who behaved as his equal. He had been raised to believe in a united kingdom over which he was destined by fate to rule, and the levers of that power were in London. Therefore it was to London that James or Charles must go. The establishment of an independent Scotland was a dream, but not one dreamed by either James or Charles Stuart.

Chapter 5

He would have forced Catholicism on Britain

This is almost certainly untrue. Charles applied the same principle to religion that his father had applied to the philosophy of Fenelon. That is to say, he adopted the course of least resistance and the one which would cause himself as little trouble as possible. It was said of him in 1745 that he 'still had his religion to seek'.

We have seen that on his triumphant entry to Edinburgh, when he had the power and opportunity to impose his own will on the religion of the populace, he insisted that the status quo be maintained and that all the Protestant services continued uninterrupted. This was not out of a sense of religious tolerance but out of hard-headed politics, since most of the Highland chiefs were non-jurant Anglicans, although their clansmen were often Catholics whose religion was quietly tolerated by their superiors. Thus he ensured that his supporters' religious beliefs were respected.

His Protestant supporters, Episcopalian or not, must have had grave doubts as to their continued freedom if James, in person, took the crown. In a draft of a letter in 1741 James said that he had no thought of assuming the Government on the same footing as his family had left it, and that he would tolerate Dissenters and maintain the Church of England. The thought of Charles as regent for such a rule was only just tolerable, and the Prince was sufficiently politically aware to ensure that the question was never openly asked.

This leaves one in ignorance as to what Charles's own beliefs were. There can be no doubt that he was raised in the deepest bosom of the Roman Catholic faith. From his father's abandonment of life as 'Jamie the Rover' the entire family was under the ever-watchful eyes of the Vatican, and his education was carefully supervised. Even as non-ecclesiastic a subject as geometry was taught to him by a monk, Father Rovillas, so his acquaintance with the science of the time, the works of Galileo and the humanism of Erasmus would have been all but non-existent.

The physical education at which he excelled was the normal routine for a nobleman's son. It included horsemanship, fencing, archery and hunting. Charles was an expert horseman and a keen shot from horseback with either musket or crossbow. He was cheered as he rode through the Piazza Navona, taking aim at open windows with his (hopefully unloaded) crossbow.

Politically his education seemed to have been limited and made few concessions to a boy training for kingship. He was aware that his grandfather had lost three kingdoms for his adherence to Rome, and he knew that the finance necessary for his father to maintain a court came mainly from the Vatican and other Catholic monarchs, but he managed to keep a low profile, playing the part of a headstrong but spiritually obedient youth for the benefit of the papacy.

The tyrannical influence of his mother steered him away from the established Church, since her near mania had driven her in no small way to her early death, while his brother, who outpaced him intellectually, embraced the Church to the extent of finally receiving the red hat of a cardinal.

It would therefore be unsurprising if Charles had turned apostate and rejected the Church and all its dogmas. Instead he managed to conceal his loathing for religious ceremonies – he much preferred the military variety – as far as would please his supporters and deny fuel to his detractors.

After the failure of the '45 he had no further need to conceal his position and he acted with self-gratification overriding all other needs. In 1748 he sent envoys to Frederick the Great to apply for Frederick's sister's hand in marriage. The prospect of an alliance with one of the richest and most powerful Protestant families in Europe was immensely attractive. Had he been accepted, which he unsurprisingly was not, he would have had to make a public renunciation of Catholicism, which would have caused him no anguish at all, since he would be rejecting his family links with Rome and its financial dependency on the papacy.

In as far as Charles thought about religion, he rejected what has been called 'theological writhings' as arid medieval intellectualism, and Charles Edward was no intellectual. He did, however, see himself as a daring plotter and secret agent, and so on 13 September 1750 he travelled to London under heavy disguise. Unfortunately he soon discovered that the English Jacobites were better at drinking brave toasts and making tearful boasts of loyalty to absent kings than at forming coherent plans and military strategies. He quickly saw that there was no realistic chance of a Jacobite rising but realised that if one did arise then his Catholicism was a drawback. And so, at an Anglican church in the Strand, now called St Mary-le-Strand, Charles Edward Stuart underwent a service of apostasy and became a communicant of the Church of England. Less than ten days later he was in Boulogne.

Robert Gordon, Bishop of London, may have conducted the confirmation. Nearly 20 years later the bishop declared that Charles had once told him that in Rome he was regarded as a firm Protestant while in Britain he was a rank papist. Charles also confided that when he was 11 or 12 years old he had 'put questions to his pedagogues' and found their answers so unsatisfactory that they 'rivetted me in my resolution of a change'.

This confirmation in the Church of England and abandonment of Rome was probably the first time in Charles's life that he undertook a major decision to please people other than himself, and the long-term result of this action was not to his liking. Having learnt of this apostasy on the death of Charles's father in 1766, Pope Clement XIII flatly refused to acknowledge him as King Charles III.

In 1771 Charles set about further plans for a marriage. As a 50-year-old Prince with no fortune his choices were limited, but he eventually settled on the 20-year-old Louise de Stolberg. Charles had also calculated that if he was married according to the Catholic rite, then the new pope, now Clement XIV, might recognise his title as Charles III. He knew that other European monarchs were waiting to follow the papal lead, and on 17 April 1772 he was married according to the Roman rite by Cardinal Marefoschi in

Macerata, the cardinal's own fief near Rome. Charles was now a Catholic again.

Although Louise professed no regard for established religion, eight years of marriage to Charles resulted in her decamping to a convent, as his mother had done. The result of this separation was a papal divorce in 1784.

Charles's final contact with the Church came about in 1788 when he was paralysed by a stroke, and on the morning of 30 January he received the last rites from his cardinal brother Henry. He was buried in the cathedral of Frascati.

It might seem that the Prince had come full circle, but since he had no choice in the place of his birth or his death he was the victim of circumstance rather than of personal devotion. He had observed the religion of those around him, giving no offence and not much caring if he gave a false impression. Thus everyone in his company presumed that his beliefs coincided with theirs and that he would act in their religious interests.

In fact he worked in no one's interest but his own. To Charles Edward, God was yet another bystander.

Chapter 6

He was let down by France

Charles Edward certainly thought so, and in his mono-maniacal logic he would seem to have had just reason. France had, he believed, pledged to help his bid for the British throne by launching a diversionary attack on England while supplying him with arms and men. In fact the reverse was true. The French planned an invasion of England to effect a regime change in London, and to facilitate this they were pre-pared to give limited aid to Charles so that he could launch what they thought of as a diversionary raid in Scotland. But Charles's mind dealt in absolutes and any indication of help, no matter how embedded in qualifications, he interpreted as total support.

The seeds of the idea of raising the Highlands had been planted in the Palazzo Muti with the arrival in 1738 of John Gordon of Glenbucket, who brought news that the Highlands were alive with revolutionary fervour and that the time was ripe for an invasion of England coinciding with the raising of the clans. James's reaction was typically cautious. He sent William Hay on an exploratory mission to Scotland and William MacGregor of Balhaldy to Paris.

By 1742 Charles was past his majority and a plan was made that he should go to Paris as soon as the French declared war on Britain. But to say that France dragged her feet is like saying that glaciers could move more rapidly. Louis XV was totally under the influence of Cardinal Fleury, who had been the king's tutor since 1715 and who echoed his English counterpart Walpole's philosophy of *'quieta non movere'* or 'let sleeping dogs lie'. In other words, 'do nothing'. Fleury died in 1743, however, and Louis decided to be his own foreign minister. Unfortunately he did not always have the Council of State uniformly behind him, and one of the reasons for French vacillations during the '45 was this lack of a cohesive policy.

Louis was lobbied by John Murray of Broughton, who reported on the supposed fervour already existing in the Scottish Highlands for the overthrow of George II. Sir Watkin Williams Wynn reported on Jacobite support in Wales, and Sir John Hynde Cotton with Lord Barrymore spoke for England. A spy for the French, James Butler, gave a glowing report to Louis on the strength of Jacobite support in England, and reluctantly Louis started to plan for an invasion of England. It was to be a surprise, secret attack without a formal declaration of war. He sent an emissary, Balhaldy, back to Rome to sound out James's commitment but gave him no letters of introduction. James was, rightly, suspicious, but Charles was determined to act and on 8 January 1744 he had his last dinner alone with his father, and after an hour's conversation he left secretly for Paris.

On 8 February Charles arrived in Paris, somewhat travel-stained after a one-month journey of disguises and deceptions. The Comte de Saxe had been ready with an invasion force waiting for the French fleet, now in Brest, to cover his crossing of the Channel. Nearly 70 years later Napoleon Bonaparte would say, 'Give me the English Channel for a few hours and I will give you Europe.' The English Jacobites, who had asked Saxe to cross unprotected in fishing boats, now wanted to wait for another parliament to focus political unrest. The Brest fleet wanted to engage the English sea-power under Sir John Norris, then detach a sub-fleet to escort Saxe across the Channel, while the English Jacobites wanted Saxe, at some unspecified time in the future, to land not at Maldon in Essex but at Blackwall nearer London. Co-ordination had never been a strong point with the Jacobites and now confusion reigned.

Saxe was gravely ill with dropsy, a symptom of heart disease and regarded in the eighteenth century as a death sentence. He was keen for action of some kind, though, especially as his presence in the area was as an overture to an invasion of the Austrian Netherlands as part of the war of the Austrian Succession. Under orders from Paris, however, he waited to embark his troops at Dunkirk while Charles, brimming with confidence, established himself at Gravelines a few miles to the west. The news of Charles's arrival meant that the French intentions were now clear to Westminster, and on 25 February 1744 George II put England on a state of invasion readiness. All elements of surprise had vanished with the Prince's much-heralded arrival on the Channel coast.

The restoration of the Stuarts was of secondary importance to Louis, who was locked into confrontation with England as his principal opponent in the war where he opposed the succession of Maria Theresa to the Holy Roman Empire. Maria Theresa was supported by Hanover, the Dutch Republic and

England, although England was probably subconsciously carrying on its age-old quarrel with Catholic France, who felt that the restoration of the Stuarts would cover their true motive of the domination of the Hapsburgs. The bizarre collection of often conflicting and certainly selfish underlying motives has led this makeshift alliance of Protestant countries to be named the Pragmatic Alliance. Charles Edward was too vain to see it as anything but serving his own personal ambitions. To the French he was no more than an excuse.

The two fleets met for indecisive skirmishes in the Channel until two great storms in March forced the French fleet, sailing out of Brest, to run back for cover. The storms also wrecked 12 of Saxe's transports, seven of them with all hands. The threatened invasion was now an impossibility and could not be re-attempted since the storms did no damage to the English fleet sheltering on the Sussex shore. With heavy irony Charles wrote to Saxe that he presumed that these had been Protestant winds. He never again wholly trusted the French.

At the request of Louis XV, who was terrified that something, unspecified, would happen, the Prince was instructed to remain in Gravelines. With his normal reactions to instructions, he disobeyed flagrantly and made visits to Paris, technically incognito. However, his presence was an open secret and his idea of incognito was attending the opera, dutifully masked, but wearing the sash and star of the Order of the Garter and raising his mask to acknowledge the applause of the audience.

Throughout 1744 and the early part of 1745 he was receiving constant reports that the Highlands were at boiling point, although a contrary point of view was emphasised by

John Murray of Broughton, who argued against impetuous action. Charles, however, disregarded any information that did not coincide with his own aspirations, and he hoped to force Louis's hand by raising the Scottish clans and then demanding French help. This was a complete misjudgement of Louis who, like himself, did not respond at all to demands even if from entirely different motives. Louis now had no intention of invading England directly but still held out hope that he would support a successful rising by Jacobites in the Highlands.

Louis also had other matters to occupy his mind. On 11 May Saxe had met the English army under Sir John Cope at Fontenay and defeated him, thus allowing Louis to relax whatever slight involvement he may have had in Stuart restoration. Concentrating troops for this battle had meant that the mainland of England was temporarily deprived of military forces, and this knowledge spurred the Prince to new efforts. After frantic negotiations he managed to acquire two ships, the *Elizabeth* and the *Doutelle*, and on 22 June 1745 he sailed. He had some vague and unwritten promises dependent on actions yet to take place, and had little money and no troops or military artefacts. In fact, he was without any concrete support from France.

The contemporary historian Frank McLynn has stated that one would search in vain for any sign of a long-term or cohesive French foreign policy towards Charles during this period. A French embassy to Charles did arrive on 14 October in the person of the Marquis d'Eguilles. Charles managed to persuade the clansmen that this was the start of French support, but the good marquis was only on a reconnaissance mission. He was impressed with Charles's progress to date, but the French wanted to be absolutely sure that they would be not only backing the winning side but also supporting a meaningful diversion. Charles thought that they were hesitating before providing a diversion to allow his total victory.

As a result of the victory of Prestonpans and encouraging reports from d'Eguilles, Louis was persuaded that as a diversionary action the Jacobite effort should not be allowed to fail. He formalised his support and signed the Treaty of Fontainebleau on 24 October 1745, allying France to the Jacobite cause. France now had further reason to support the Jacobite cause since the Royal Navy threatened her colonial trade and had virtually strangled the French East India Company, thus beginning the activity which would lead to the final expulsion of France from India. The opportunity for a strike against England was hugely attractive, and Louis started to contemplate actual involvement in an invasion of England.

As a result, a glimmer of hope did come to the Jacobite army when they were at their furthermost advance into England, at Derby. Louis sent his favourite, the Duc de Richelieu, with 15,000 men to assemble an invading army at the Channel ports. In a similar strategy to that which had failed so spectacularly under Marshal Saxe, Richelieu made firm plans to cross the Channel in a fleet of fishing boats to coincide with the Jacobite advance on London. These faded when on 16 December Charles, on the advice from his Council of War, failed to continue the advance and the Jacobite army turned north to retreat towards Scotland.

Given the speed of communications the French were taken totally by surprise. They had planned the onslaught for 29 December, and Richelieu had left Paris for the coast on 23 December. On the 29th he received the news of the retreat from Derby. There was also no sign of a rising by the English Jacobites.

More damaging were the successful attacks by the English fleet under Admiral Vernon on Richelieu's transport ships. Richelieu's temper was not improved by the somewhat surprising arrival of Charles's brother Henry, whose constant piety, praying and genuflections annoyed the grossly profligate duke. Since the immensely rich Richelieu, a great-nephew of Louis XIII's cardinal, was the most notorious libertine and lecher in France, thought to be the model for the rake and serial seducer Valmont in Choderlos de Laclos's *Les Liaisons Dangereuses*, this was hardly surprising. Almost as annoying were Henry's totally unnecessary warnings about the strength of Vernon and the Royal Navy. Richelieu's already short temper was at breaking point.

Richelieu maintained the hope of invasion through the setbacks of storms and English depredations, even contemplating an invasion of Cornwall while the Jacobite army plodded its way north. Ironically, as Richelieu abandoned his efforts news came of the Jacobite victory at Falkirk. But this was too late and of no real military advantage to a cross-Channel invasion.

The French still intended to support Charles, and a force was assembled by the Duc de Fitzjames, of which three companies arrived in Aberdeen in early 1746. They were the last physical reinforcements to reach Charles, since the Duke of Cumberland's advance into Scotland forestalled any hope of success.

There was now no further hope of reinforcements from France, although some temporary successes provoked vain hopes of France recognising Scotland as an independent nation. These hopes were founded more on the emptying of brandy bottles than on political reality, and after Culloden Louis could reassure himself that he had not spilt a drop of French blood or spent a single louis d'or in support of a losing side.

He did, however, feel a certain loyalty to an enemy of England, and there were some half-hearted and inept attempts to rescue Charles before his final escape on a French warship, the aptly named *L'Heureux*, in October 1746.

Charles was tolerated in uneasy exile until September 1750, when he left France for the last time. In his disillusion he felt that he had been first ignored and then given false hope by a Catholic monarch. By the end of the month Charles, secretly in London, had embraced the Church of England, for purely political reasons.

He undoubtedly felt let down by France since he was certain for most of his life that everyone agreed with him and would work exclusively for his cause. He never understood that Louis – when he did anything at all – served France's interests first and that Charles's ambitions were only to be supported when they could be used to France's advantage. Charles was not let down by France since they had interest only in the restoration of the Stuarts as a means of defeating England. Charles's gifts for self-delusion meant that he was let down only by a reality he was incapable of grasping.

Chapter 7

At Derby he turned back out of cowardice

This cannot be held to be in any way true. Charles's personal courage had never been in doubt. Although it had not been put to the test in open battle, his bravery as a huntsman and his behaviour on the march from Glenfinnan to Edinburgh had shown him to be physically fit enough to lead a major campaign. But in October 1745 he was in Edinburgh with all Scotland under his control. The castles of Edinburgh, Stirling and Dumbarton were still held by Hanoverian forces, but they could be circumvented until he had siege machinery, or until starvation drove them to surrender. He held court in the capital, and the citizenry flocked to be part of it. It was true to say that the Stuart restoration was successfully established, at least in the popular mind of Scotland.

But this was a hollow victory, since Charles's personal ambition was to regain the throne of Britain, nominally for his father. So this campaign must be regarded as only stage one, with the precise strategy for stage two yet to be decided.

If he stayed still in Edinburgh then his Highland army would trickle back to its home as the Government gathered its seasoned troops in the south for an invasion. This was clearly not an option in either strategic or practical terms. Alternatively he could lead his army back north, while maintaining discipline, and give it time to regroup. In the Highlands he could hope for further recruitment in the spring and a greater appointment of officers. The clan regiments had simply followed their chiefs or lairds who had no practical experience in eighteenth-century warfare. He could hope for reinforcements from France, and following Prestonpans his relations with d'Eguilles were excellent. D'Eguilles had brought encouragement and some volunteer officers who, unfortunately, were the sort of opportunistic adventurers who would volunteer for anything to their advantage. One such was Richard Warren, who after six months with the Jacobites returned to France to 'report'. So glowing was his fictitious report that he was rewarded with a baronetcy, and he returned to Scotland the next year as a ship's captain.

Charles's third alternative was to continue what had been his triumphal march south and invade England, occupy London, oust the Whig administration and occupy the throne as his father's regent. Against him was General Wade, who had arrived in Newcastle at the end of October, his ranks swollen with Dutch reinforcements. Sir John Cope was in Berwick but was ordered to join Wade, and a third force under Lord Ligonier was to defend a line from Nottingham to Chester. Ligonier was unhappy at the vagueness of his command, but since the target for a possible attack was not known, it could be nothing else. Meanwhile, exhausted regiments were being withdrawn from the Netherlands, and even Swiss mercenaries were engaged. London had no firm idea of the Jacobite strength, but the speed of the advance through

Scotland had alarmed them. Military intelligence was in its infancy and such knowledge was rare, although there was a small network operating on behalf of the Government. The Jacobites had none.

Charles was aware that he had far superior forces ranged against him but he would have the advantage of the initiative if he acted quickly, and on the evening of 30 October 1745 a War Council met in Edinburgh. Undoubtedly the most influential member of this council was the 59-year-old Lord George Murray, Charles's Lieutenant-General and principal adviser. Had there been sufficient forces, Murray would have argued for an immediate advance into England after Prestonpans, while Charles's delay had allowed the Government forces time to breathe again. Unfortunately Charles did not have what George Murray considered to be sufficient forces.

Charles, however, was strongly in favour of a rapid pursuit of Cope to Newcastle where he felt he could win a decisive battle. Murray pointed out that he had far too few disciplined troops to engage in a set-piece battle. Since Murray was a veteran of wars in Flanders as well as the '15 and the abortive rising in 1719, his views prevailed over Charles's bravado, and Murray went on to recommend a withdrawal to the Highlands.

This resulted in a lengthy debate, with most of the clan chiefs supporting Murray, but eventually, and by only one vote, the decision was made to invade. Next the choice of route was discussed. Murray pointed out that proceeding south towards Kelso would give the Hanoverians no clue and would allow them no room for manoeuvre. The Jacobite army could then turn to its right and aim for Carlisle. The rugged mountain country of Cumberland would suit the Highland troops and hinder the more formally trained Hanoverian forces.

Thus on 5 November the Jacobite army left Dalkeith to the south of Edinburgh for an advance into England. They would march south to Jedburgh, which could be used as a starting-off point for Newcastle, then diverge to the south-west, at which point the route of invasion would be clear to the Hanoverians. The army numbered about 5,500, with 5,000 infantry and 500 cavalry. The cavalry was divided into five squadrons. They also had an artillery detachment of 13 guns of varying small sizes, none large enough for siege work and in fact more of a hindrance than a help. The infantry were led by Lord George's Atholl Brigade of 1,000 men, and the remainder were led by their chiefs and lairds, divided between Highlanders and Lowlanders. All could be classified as pressed men, either through feudal duty or clan loyalty, although the relatively low rate of desertion shows how efficient these ties were. The only truly volunteer men were in the Edinburgh Regiment, recruited from the slums in the hope of fortune by John Roy Stewart, a veteran of Europe where he had fought for the French at Fontenoy. He has been described by one contemporary historian as the very epitome of a Jacobite adventurer – in other words, a mercenary of unbridled rapacity.

The army marched barefoot, clad in plaids or trews, and was lamentably ill-equipped. Most men carried a basket-hilt broadsword or claymore and a dirk or dagger. There were some muskets and bayonets of varying ages and effectiveness, but there was a distinct shortage of round shot and powder.

They would rely to a large extent on what could be captured in successful engagements. Similarly the commissary was slight and would be supplied as the advance proceeded. This lack was exacerbated by the loss of tents, stores and ammunition due to the clumsy fording of a stream at Moffat. The army would now have to rely on billeting, thus causing hostility among the locals, and once their meagre stores of ammunition ran out they would only have what they captured in battle.

There was a shipment of arms and cash from Spain, although it was no more than a token contribution, and Charles still had hopes of help either from France or from a spontaneous rising by the English Jacobites.

The force made good enough progress, crossing into England on 8 November at the River Esk, where we are told that the Highlanders drew their swords, did an about-turn to face Scotland and saluted their homeland. Unfortunately this fine gesture was spoiled by Lochiel cutting himself in the process – an evil omen for the superstitious Highlanders.

A more tangible threat stood in their way, however, in the shape of the castle of Carlisle. Accepting the advice of Lord George, and trying to ignore the fact that siege work was not a strong point with the clansmen, there was no option but to commence a siege on 9 November. Further south, the Hanoverians were in a state of confusion, with Wade being commanded to liaise with the lords-lieutenant in the neighbouring counties, while Ligonier was to place himself under Wade's command (300 miles away!) and to block the Highlanders' advance south by establishing himself in Chester. Unfortunately Ligonier had not yet left London.

Charles, in keeping with the best precepts of medieval war and what he had witnessed in his brief visit to the siege of Gaeta, sent a message to the Mayor of Carlisle saying that if he surrendered, the town would not be sacked. He received no reply and the siege began. On 12 November Charles was informed that his continual cannonade had only killed a single cow, and he wanted to withdraw and face Wade. On advice from Lord George the siege continued, and Charles's advance to meet Wade was halted by foul snowy weather. By the 15th it became clear that neither side could claim a total victory, and the city surrendered to the Jacobites. The 72-year-old Wade had never left Newcastle, but a disastrous event had taken place among the Jacobites. Lord George had resigned his position as Lieutenant-General.

The given reason was the slight that Lord George felt he had suffered when the surrender of Carlisle had been accepted by the Duke of Perth and Murray of Broughton, Charles's secretary and a bitter rival of his namesake. This threatened to cause a split in the Jacobites' ever fissiparous ranks, and a compromise deal was negotiated whereby Perth was given command of the baggage train, and Murray of Broughton was removed from the War Council. Charles's troops entered the town and began collecting foodstuffs and acquiring lodgings, although the Atholl men under Lord George were uncomfortably lodged in the castle cellars, which they set about emptying.

Wade's forces were no better off, with many still exhausted from the journey from Flanders and the foreign mercenaries dispirited with the freezing weather. Also, dysentery was starting to break out, and the elderly Wade was a notorious miser. This meant that the men were barely surviving on poverty rations. He marched on Hexham and the men had to sleep in the open since they could not pitch tents on the frozen ground, and Wade would not buy straw or kindling for cooking fires.

On 18 November Charles made a triumphal entry into Carlisle, a ceremony at which he excelled, but had to face opposition in the Council. Lord George, having returned to his command, used his reacquired position to insist that the invasion cease and the army return to Scotland. Charles's effective strength, after casualties, desertion and the need to garrison Carlisle, was now down to 4,500, while behind him Edinburgh was in the process of being retaken, and the Royal Navy's iron grip on the Channel made French intervention there more and more unlikely. Charles countered these arguments by saying that as they entered Lancashire they would enter Jacobite country, and he claimed to have letters from them proposing to join forces with him at Preston. The forces were, in fact, fictitious. He also said that if d'Eguilles reported a withdrawal then all hope of French support would wither. Broughton had been allowed to join the meeting to report on finance and he reported that the Jacobite position could only be maintained by raising further finance from the south. Lord George backed down and the decision was made to continue the advance.

While preparations for the onward advance were being made in Carlisle, Wade returned to Newcastle, having achieved nothing except to shatter the morale of his exhausted troops. Further south, Ligonier at last left London and started a movement north. By 19 November his advance guard was in Chester. London, still defending on the back foot, had no clear idea of where the Jacobites meant to launch their major attack. They might be intending to attack London, although with such a small force this seemed unlikely, or they might be aiming for the south coast where they could hope to receive massive French reinforcements, or they could take to the Welsh hills, the type of country to which they were accustomed, and seek support from Welsh Jacobites. Any response would need speed of manoeuvre, a tactic at which neither Ligonier nor Wade was showing any expertise.

Charles's army was showing such speed that by 30 November, St Andrew's Day, they made yet another triumphal entry, this time into Manchester. They had travelled over 200 miles in ten days, an average of 20 miles daily. The speed of this advance distressed many of the clansmen who were not used to extensive travel. In fact many had never travelled further than on raids a few miles from their own homes. Their furious energy came in short bursts of wild activity and they had not developed the slow stamina of regular troops. Charles made the journey on foot at the head of his men although he was occasionally to be seen leaning on a supporting shoulder.

The Lancastrian Jacobites of the Midlands, as prophesied by Lord George, failed to materialise, but there was little opposition to the incursion, and crowds turned out to see the Young Pretender and his band of exotic savages pass by. It was often a circus atmosphere, and there is a legend, probably true, that one Sergeant Dickson asked permission to march ahead and enter Manchester with a drummer to seek out recruits. Accompanied by his mistress and to the beat of a drum, he entered the town. The Jacobite sympathisers rallied to him and he enlisted 180 men. Some legends are just too good to debunk.

In Manchester there was another crucial meeting of the War Council, where the subject was, once again, whether or not to continue. The Welsh support promised by Sir Watkin Williams Wynn had failed to appear, but Charles, who inevitably was for further rapid advances, was supported by David Morgan, a Welsh Jacobite. Lord George agreed to give the English Jacobites under Lord Barrymore a last chance to appear, adding that if they did not then the only course of action would be retreat. Charles ignored this and the army set out for Stockport.

The Government, at last despairing of Lord Ligonier's lack of activity, sent him to the Netherlands and replaced him with the Duke of Cumberland, the 23-year-old younger son of George II. He marched the Hanoverian army west to cut off any possible alliance of the Jacobites with their non-existent Welsh supporters. However, by 4 December the Jacobite army was in Derby, about 130 miles from London and therefore only seven days' march away.

Wade and Cumberland were far away, unable to intercept a headlong dash by the Jacobites. Cumberland was in Stafford, and Wade, with his usual tardiness, had got no further south than Wetherby in Yorkshire.

In Derby the Prince was lodged at Exeter House in Full Street, where he dined lavishly with his officers and discussed the method of his entry into London. Lord George, notably, did not join in the general merriment. The town echoed to the Jacobite army, at last having something to celebrate, holding parties and drinking until dawn. Next morning an order went out for a Jacobite Council of War, but first the profoundly hung-over army worshipped together at All Saints Collegiate Church, before the colonels met in council at the George Inn. According to Lord George, Councils of War were now seldom held since they nearly always contradicted Charles's intentions, and this one was no different. To Charles the situation seemed straightforward. London lay ahead of them like a ripe plum ready to be picked and all they had to do was march on and pick it. Lord George Murray, on the other hand, remembered his advice at Manchester – that if no support arrived from English or Welsh Jacobites, then retreat was their only option. He pointed out that with two regular armies at their rear and a well-trained militia numbering 9,000 men awaiting them at Finchley, they were in a most vulnerable situation. If they met Cumberland's army in battle and even if they defeated him, which was by no means certain, their strength would be reduced by at least 1,000 men and they would represent easy pickings for the militia. Survival depended on a disciplined retreat.

Charles, now apparently in a state of denial, responded by discussing which regiments should lead the victory parade. The clan chiefs, however, started to wonder if his aim was solely to restore his family, without any regard for the future of Scotland, and the afternoon debate became more vituperative and Charles more isolated.

In the evening one Dudley Bradstreet, a Hanoverian prisoner, was introduced. He was a deserter from Cumberland and came with the disquieting news that there was a third army, under Ligonier and General Henry Hawley, with 9,000 more men, at Northampton and ready to move. This turned disquiet into panic and a vote was taken, with Charles now alone in advocating continuing. The decision was clear and orders for a retreat were given.

This was on 6 December 1745, still remembered by sentimental Jacobite supporters as 'Black Friday', and the army started to move out at 7 a.m. By the evening of 20 December they were once again on Scottish soil, where Charles could consider a return campaign.

They had retreated around 300 miles in two weeks, while the advance had lasted from 8 November until 4 December, 28 days in all. This advance had included the siege of Carlisle and various skirmishes, and had taken place in a spirit of optimism, with the Prince on foot leading his army. On the return he rode, head down, at the rear of his dispirited army. Even among his supporters the fact that he was now frequently drunk began to cause disquiet.

Lord George now held the reality of command, although he had the troublesome task of ensuring the safe return of the now practically useless artillery train. He managed to hold the forces together, although this time there was more looting and misbehaviour by the Highlanders. His scouting parties to the rear meant that he could always feel safe from surprise by the pursuing Cumberland. They had met little opposition on the march, with the now decrepit and exhausted Wade almost static in Yorkshire. On the western side of England, the more energetic Cumberland suffered from the disadvantage always experienced by a pursuer, that the pursued held the initiative.

The two armies did meet in an extended skirmish at Clifton, just north of Shap summit in modern Cumbria, when the Highlanders charged into Cumberland's dismounted dragoons, inflicting dreadful casualties, but Murray allowed the survivors to flee across the moors. Cumberland reached Carlisle on 20 December, only to find that Charles's army was safely back in Scotland. The tiny garrison, mainly of the Manchester Regiment, was swiftly overcome and Colonel Townley, the Jacobite commander, surrendered. Contrary to custom, he, along with nine other officers including the chaplain, then suffered the medieval penalty of hanging, castrating and disembowelling while still alive, then being cut into four pieces, or 'quartering'. Perhaps a hint of the barbarity to come.

Cumberland was recalled to the south to take care of defences against a French invasion. Over a week later, on 29 December, the news of Charles's retreat from Derby reached the Duc de Richelieu in Boulogne and the idea of a French invasion was abandoned. Murray had already returned to Scotland and the retreat from Derby was complete. As an example of the disciplined retreat of a large army it was, thanks to him, a military triumph. But had this decision to retreat been taken wisely?

As we have seen, the Jacobite army possessed no intelligence service, and even the battle-hardened Lord George used no spy network, so their summary of the situation at Derby was derived from rumour and guesswork. Dudley Bradstreet was in fact a spy planted to bring misinformation to Charles, and his loyalties were to Cumberland. He was a double agent. There was no third army under Hawley. Cumberland's army numbered no more than 4,000 men, who were exhausted by poor quartering and forced winter marches. Their fate at the hands of 5,500 pumped-up Highlanders can only be guessed at. The much-vaunted 9,000 Finchley militia were in reality a poorly trained, inexperienced and unwillingly recruited 4,000, most of whom would have deserted and who would have been easily brushed aside by the Jacobites.

In London itself the population were heartily sick of the venality of the Whig supremacy in Parliament, and the Tories would have welcomed Charles as a breath of fresh air. The Government had made no specific preparations to fortify the city, concentrating instead on rushing forces to the Channel.

The only cowardice Charles showed at Derby was in bowing to the overwhelming opinions of his War Council, and it is likely that had his view prevailed he would have been able to seize a London terrified into supine inaction by the savage reputation of the Highlanders.

Restoring the Catholic monarchy of the Stuarts would have required political negotiation with Parliament of the subtlest and most delicate kind, and whether Charles or his father were capable of this is doubtful in the extreme. Charles did not lose his determination to take the capital. Nor did he drop the metaphorical ball with the line in sight. It was kicked out of his hands.

Chapter 8

The loyal Scots were butchered by an English army at Culloden

Charles had no intention of luring Cumberland into a set-piece battle on Drumossie Moor, near Culloden House, when he followed his retreating army into Scotland across the River Esk on 20 December 1745. Reflecting that he had invaded England and returned with the loss of only 24 men he could congratulate himself, even if the purpose of the invasion had never been near achievement. His immediate plan was to advance to Stirling from where the clansmen and others would disperse to their homelands before a recall in the spring. Then, with French help gained through d'Eguilles, he would return to England as soon as possible.

He entered Glasgow on 26 December, lodging at Shawfield House, now part of the Trongate, and changed from his campaigning dress into his more sumptuous French attire. He held balls, as well as, of course, a military review on Glasgow Green. Once again he was 'Bonnie Prince Charlie'. But a new player had entered the game.

He was Lieutenant-General Henry Hawley, a 66-year-old career soldier and newly appointed Commander-in-Chief in Scotland, replacing the ageing and ineffectual Wade on

20 December 1745. He was a veteran of the war of the Spanish Succession, fighting at Almanza in Spain in 1707, in Scotland at Sheriffmuir, and in Europe on the winning side at Dettingen and the losing side at Fontenoy. Henry Hawley was a severe battle-hardened tyrant, whose troops, according to his brigade-major James Wolfe, 'dread his severity, hate the man and hold his military knowledge in contempt'. His men cringeingly nicknamed him 'Lord Chief Justice' and he would soon gain another nickname as 'Hangman' Hawley.

He arrived in Edinburgh on 6 January and immediately stamped his personality on the city by erecting four sets of gallows: two in the city and two in the port of Leith. They were put into use at once and Hawley liked to emphasise their threat by letting the naked corpses hang for a few days. Humiliation was part of his punishment policy.

He had about 8,000 men under his command, although he had no high expectations of them. Notwithstanding that opinion, on 13 January he set out to drive the 'rascally scum' out of Stirling.

The siege of Stirling Castle had begun with the Highlanders, who were completely inexperienced in siege warfare, placing themselves under the command of one Mirabel de Gordon, a man of uncertain ancestry and a self-declared expert in siege warfare. He was held in contempt by the forces, who ironically nicknamed him Mr Admirable.

Charles, however, in accordance with the Stuart habit of valetudinarianism, had fallen ill with an unspecified illness, probably influenza. In common with many people who are habitual invalids, Charles was never ill at times of great activity, but when the tension relaxed, the exhaustion, which had previously not had time to manifest itself, took over. The Prince retired to bed – but possibly not alone.

He was lodging with Sir Hugh Paterson at Bannockburn, and Paterson's 25-year-old niece, Clementina Walkinshaw, was also in the house. She was the daughter of John Walkinshaw of Barrowfield. A wealthy Glasgow merchant and Jacobite, he had been captured at Sheriffmuir and had escaped and been subsequently pardoned. His daughter's names – Clementina Maria Sophia, echoing Charles's mother – betray his affiliations and she was largely educated on the continent. Cut off thus from her family and the whirligig of engagements and assignations which would have been normal for such a wealthy heiress, she felt herself to be lonely and overlooked. Now, for the tall and prepossessing Clementina to have her father's hero and her romantic idol in a bed in the same house and needing her care must have been a romantic dream near to coming true. An exchange of flirtations there must certainly have been although we can have no certainty as to their extent.

They were brought to an abrupt end when news came to Charles that Hawley had moved his army to Linlithgow and was preparing to do battle. Hawley's idea of victory was the total annihilation of the enemy and he was confident that he would 'brush aside this savage undisciplined rabble'.

The rabble did not wait to be annihilated, and on 14 January the freshly reinforced and remustered Jacobite army of now some 8,000 men drew up at Bannockburn. Hawley was still some way off, and somewhat despondently and having no one to fight, the Jacobites disbanded. Three days later Lord George suggested taking up battle positions on a ridge to the south of Falkirk. Charles, for once, concurred and the Jacobites moved into battle formation. Hawley watched the movement with some disdain and, concluding that such ill-trained troops would be some time in forming ranks, he went to lunch with Lady Kilmarnock at Callendar House.

Urgent news that the Jacobites were nearly in full possession of the high ground brought Hawley from the table with his lunch uneaten. Hatless and with a napkin still around his neck he commanded his cavalry forward. Contrary to their normal manoeuvres of a charge across level ground to terrify the infantry, followed by regular exchanges of musketry between the closing sides, the cavalry were now forced to advance diagonally uphill towards the Highlanders who, under strict orders from Lord George, held their fire until the horsemen were at pistol range. This coolness was not the response Hawley had expected. By four o'clock and in driving rain, Lord George gave the signal for his troops to fire. Eighty cavalrymen died instantly. Two cavalry regiments fled, riding back downhill over their own infantry, and the third, stationary and in a state of total confusion, was attacked by the Highlanders, having thrown away their now useless muskets, screaming and wielding their targes and claymores. Targes, or targets, were round wooden shields about three feet in diameter, covered in leather and heavily studded, sometimes carrying four-inch-long spikes. Used as a weapon as well as a shield they were a fearsome sight, as were the claymores – basket-hilted broadswords with a two-inch-wide, four-foot blade. When the Highlanders charged into the astonished cavalry, horses were disembowelled before their unhorsed riders were sliced to pieces on the ground.

The Highlanders continued their avalanche of swirling blades as the remaining Hanoverian forces fled the field in terror. The still hatless Hawley and his headquarter officers were forced to withdraw rapidly to safety, before fleeing first to Linlithgow and then to recently reoccupied Edinburgh. Some of the retreating Hanoverians were reported to have overshot the capital and fled as far as Musselburgh.

Control and tactics had been solely under the guidance of Lord George, with Charles as no more than a spectator. The battle had lasted less than 20 minutes, and Hawley had lost 400 men and 20 officers as against the Jacobite losses of 50 men. Legend has it that Charles finished Hawley's uneaten lunch. So much for 'brushing the savages aside'. Hawley had never suffered such a defeat and the deep bitterness he felt towards Highlanders would have monstrous repercussions at Culloden.

Charles's illness returned and he went back to Clementina's gentle care. The siege of Stirling Castle continued unsuccessfully as Mirabel de Gordon, the French 'expert' in siege warfare, turned out to be a drunken impostor. Had Charles been able to move on Hawley immediately after Falkirk the situation could have been very different, with the possibility that Lord George could march on Edinburgh while the Prince went south with the main force. But delay was inevitable and morale fell among the now inactive Highlanders. Charles, however, was reinvigorated after his recovery from illness and felt that he now had the initiative and strength to recommence his invasion of England.

Then, on the morning of 29 January 1746 he received a letter, signed by Murray and the seven principal Highland chieftains. It offered no chance for a Stuart victory except by a withdrawal to the Highlands. A large-scale invasion of England with a diminished army and in winter conditions was not to be contemplated. But a winter rest held out the possibility of a new invasion with 10,000 men. Charles was baffled as to why, after such a victory as Falkirk, he should now retreat. The next day, news came that William Augustus, Duke of Cumberland and favourite son of George II, had arrived in Edinburgh, taking over from Hawley as supreme commander of the Hanoverian forces and bringing with him fresh troops from Europe. This was a serious intervention and showed that Westminster meant business this time. The Jacobites were not just to be repelled, they were to be crushed out of all existence.

After the initial chaos of Falkirk had died down, Hawley turned the rout into a disciplined retreat to unite with Cumberland in the east. Two days later the Jacobite army had turned north and was in Crieff, about 15 miles west of Perth, where Lord George held another War Council. He was exhausted, not only by his efforts to keep the army together but also by his constant conflict with the headstrong Prince. At the council it was decided to split the retreating army, with the Prince proceeding due north with the clansmen, and Lord George travelling east to the coast at Aberdeen, hopefully arriving on 10 February, and then going to meet up with the Prince again at Inverness.

For his part, Cumberland had no intention of invading the Highlands in the depths of winter. He had travelled to Linlithgow, where on 1 January his men accidentally and probably drunkenly burned down the old palace, birthplace of Charles's great-great-great-grandmother Mary, Queen of Scots.

On 16 January the Prince arrived at Moy Hall, south of Inverness, where he was lavishly welcomed by the 23-year-old Lady Anne Farquharson Mackintosh. Her husband Angus was asked to raise three new companies by John Campbell, Lord Loudoun, and Anne donned male attire and recruited the men from her glens herself. After Culloden these men changed sides and joined Lord Loudoun with his Hanoverian 'Black Watch'. Anne raised a further 400 men for the Jacobites from the Mackintoshes and the confederacy of Clan Chattan.

There is a theory that the name 'Chattan' comes from the 'Catti', a Gaulish tribe driven out by the Romans, but after the fifteenth century the name applied itself to a confederation of smaller clans under the overlordship of the Mackintoshes. Since women could not command in the field, Lady Anne and her men, under MacGillivray of Drumglass, joined the Prince's army at Bannockburn on 14 January. Lady Anne now joined Jacobite legend as 'Colonel Anne'.

Charles had a price of £30,000 on his head, probably today worth about £30 million, and had last lodged with one Grant of Darnalchy. Lady Anne knew that Grant was a Hanoverian supporter and would probably have informed the Government forces in Inverness as to the Prince's movements, so she mounted a guard under her blacksmith, Donald Fraser, on the road from Inverness in case of a sortie to capture the Prince. The Inverness garrison was under the command of Lord Loudoun, who had fled there after Prestonpans. Lady Anne's guard was more necessary than she knew since the Prince's erstwhile host, Darnalchy, had as Anne suspected sent word to Loudoun that Charles was travelling to Moy with only a nominal bodyguard. What followed was the very stuff of adventure novels.

Loudoun had assembled a raiding force of 1,500 men and placed a cordon around Inverness to prevent word of any activity reaching the Prince. But soldiers, when in drink, do gossip and boast to attractive ladies, and one of them told a barmaid of the proposed raid. She told the dowager Lady Mackintosh, who sent a boy messenger, Lachlan Mackintosh, barefoot to warn Lady Anne.

A local boy raised in the heather, he slipped through Loudoun's cordon with ease and brought the news to Moy Hall in the middle of the night. The result was electrifying. Lady Anne, still in her night clothes, roused the Prince and sent him, clad in dressing-gown and slippers, running through the pitch-black woods to Lochiel and his Camerons. She augmented her blacksmith's four men with more of her servants, who in the darkness pretended to be the advance guard of the Jacobite army. Fictional shouted orders were given, calling the Camerons, Clanranalds and Keppochs to stand to. A volley or two was fired towards Loudoun's men and there was much clattering and shouting by ghillies and gamekeepers. A chance shot fired at random killed Donald MacCrimmon, piper to the Macleods who had come out for the Hanoverians. Loudoun began to think that his informant had been a double agent and he was walking into a trap. He ordered his now panicking and terrified men back to Inverness.

This was the 'Rout of Moy', reported with joy by d'Eguilles as the exploits of *La Belle Rebelle*, and probably the last piece of good luck to fall the Jacobites' way. Like all their good fortunes it was not complete, since during his woodland exodus the Prince caught a cold which developed into pneumonia and scarlet fever, rendering him *hors de combat* for all of February. He convalesced in Inverness Castle and Culloden House.

The Jacobite army continued to advance, taking Inverness on 18 February, and Loudoun fled north to Tain, leaving Inverness to the Prince. Loudoun was eventually captured and given, on parole, into the care of Charles, who with a certain sense of humour transferred him to the care of Lady Anne. She greeted him as 'Your servant, Captain.' He replied, 'Your servant, Colonel.' His regiment remained a part of the Hanoverian army. Cumberland, who had met Lady Anne, was entranced by her and reported to Major-General Hawley that it was a pity that she was a rebel since she was really a very pretty woman and honour should be done to her. Hawley replied that he would honour her with a mahogany gallows and a silken rope. She subsequently met Cumberland in London and danced with him, albeit to a Jacobite tune. She died at the age of 64 in 1787.

Lord George arrived in Inverness on 19 February after a fearsome journey through snowstorms. He had been re-inforced by two French ships which docked at Aberdeen bringing 120 cavalrymen. However, two other supply ships had been taken by the Royal Navy, so the cavalrymen's horses and 400 other foot soldiers were lost to the Prince. This was the last of the much-vaunted French reinforcements Charles had been promising since Moidart. Murray set out from Inverness to capture Lord Loudoun and Duncan Forbes.

Forbes was the Lord President of the Court of Session and a staunch Hanoverian, a close ally of the ever-changing Lord Lovat, and a principal influence on the Macleods of Skye. When Charles had taken Edinburgh in the previous year Forbes had fled north to his estate at Culloden House, but was now a fugitive in Sutherland with Loudoun. Eventually the pair abandoned their soldiers and fled to Skye, where they were welcomed by the non-participating Skye men and there they sat out the rising in comfortable exile.

With the Prince for the moment out of action, Lord George felt he had a free hand to continue the campaign in a soldierly manner. The Highlanders, still in a state of elation after Falkirk, showed no sign of dispersing, but Murray was properly concerned that his situation was insecure with the fortresses on the Great Glen still in Hanoverian hands. Fort George, to the east of Inverness, soon fell, and Fort Augustus surrendered on 5 March, although the garrison blew up the magazine to prevent it falling into Jacobite hands. Fort William proved an altogether harder nut to crack. The Hanoverians had reinforced the garrison, and the Jacobites had to wait for their artillery to arrive from Fort Augustus, some 30 miles to the north. The situation was not improved when Colonel James Grant, who was in charge of the siege operations, was wounded, and control of the siege was, astonishingly, given to the inept Mirabel de Gordon. The siege fell into stalemate and the Highlanders eventually withdrew on 30 March having to abandon all their artillery. However, the taking of the two most important Highland forts made March into a month of celebration for the Jacobites, even though their prince had not been present.

Looking for fresh objectives, Murray realised that Cumberland had garrisoned Blair Castle with Scots Fusiliers and the Argyll militia. The castle was his ancestral home and he requested more troops from Charles. Not waiting for an answer, which would have been negative, he set out to retake the castle. Cumberland strengthened the garrison with fresh men under the Prince of Hesse, and Lord George was forced to withdraw.

His feeling of betrayal was exacerbated by the fact that Charles had, after seeing Lord George's string of successes with forts, allowed his ancestral home to fall, presumably out of jealousy. Charles, with typical Stuart paranoia, now increased his distrust of Lord George and had him placed under close supervision.

The situation for the Hanoverian forces had, however, improved since the defeat at Falkirk. The Duke of Cumberland had arrived as supreme commander on 31 January, and by 27 February he had established a headquarters in Aberdeen, where he rested his troops for seven weeks. Thanks to recuperation from hospitalisation, such as it was, his numbers grew to about 10,000, and his infantry was now equipped with a new type of bayonet. This fitted into a socket around the barrel of the rifle, allowing the rifle to be fired with the bayonet in place. A technique was developed to strike upwards and to the right, coming below the raised sword arm of the claymore-wielding Highlander. Cumberland was convinced that the Jacobite movement could only be stopped by 'military severity', and to the Hanoverian mind that meant total annihilation. He was disappointed that Charles had avoided an immediate confrontation. It was intended that the houses of any of those bearing arms would be destroyed as part of the 'disagreeable hunting of these wild beasts', and this was endorsed by the Prime Minister, the Duke of Newcastle. Early in March the Royal Navy harried the west coast of Scotland, burning 400 houses and barns filled with foodstuffs. Lochiel and Keppoch were appalled at this onslaught on innocent crofters and laid the blame, probably correctly, at the door of the Campbells.

The navy also dealt a tremendous blow to the Jacobites when on 25 March it captured the *Prince Charles*. This vessel had been sent from France with money, weapons and powder, but it ran aground and the crew and cargo were seized. Charles's attempts to recover his treasure were unsuccessful and the Jacobites could now rely on no further outside help.

On 16 March Cumberland sent out reconnaissance parties to scout various crossing points on the River Spey, and on 12 April he crossed the river unopposed. This was because Charles had been advised, wrongly, that the crossing points were indefensible. His new adviser, replacing Lord George, was the Irishman John O'Sullivan, one of the Seven Men of Moidart, who had acted as quartermaster throughout the campaign. His appointment, the result of the breakdown of Charles's relationship with Lord George, was a disaster for the campaign.

Three days later, on 15 April, his 25th birthday, Cumberland crossed the River Nairn and awaited the arrival of pre-planned reinforcements brought unopposed by a naval flotilla. Charles had arrived at Culloden House on the previous afternoon, but the Jacobite army was still in a state of confusion. Charles had despatched an ineffective force of

1,500 men on a wild-goose chase into Caithness, while his relationship with Lord George had reached breaking point. In fact, as we have seen, Lord George had been replaced in the Prince's favours. Realising that a possibly conclusive battle with Cumberland was now inevitable, Charles tried to seize the initiative by choosing the ground best suited to his forces.

Lord George had chosen a place north-east of Culloden House, where the Highlanders could occupy a ridge from which they could launch a downhill charge similar to that which had been so successful at Falkirk. Below the ridge there was little room for Cumberland to deploy his artillery and cavalry. But Charles sent O'Sullivan to verify the choice and he rejected it in favour of an open field near Culloden House. It was marshy and flat, which would impede the Highlanders' charge. It also provided an open field of fire for the artillery and cavalry. In other words, it was a killing field. On O'Sullivan's advice Charles decided on it as a suitable place to station his troops.

On the afternoon of 14 April Charles arrived at Culloden House but did not go to bed. Instead he had to review his situation, a task made more difficult by feuding among the higher command. The condition of the Jacobite army was poor. Many men had left for their villages and would not return for some days. The army was lacking in pay and, due to the sudden sickness of Murray of Broughton (the officer in charge of provisions, who had been replaced by the unfortunately incompetent John Hay of Restalrig), was not being properly fed, existing on half rations of oatmeal, although there were plentiful foodstuffs unused in Inverness.

Charles, at last and too late, decided to take the initiative and attack Cumberland while his forces were still celebrating their commander's birthday. This meant that the now starving Jacobite army spent 15 April in a state of readiness for an attack that never came. Lord George, to appease his over-eager Prince, suggested a night attack on Cumberland's camp where surprise might give him an advantage. Instead of a meal, the troops were issued with a biscuit each and set off at midnight, but took over an hour to cover six miles. They avoided what roads there were and stumbled and collapsed in the pitch-dark morass. To ease the march they carried no muskets but would rely on claymores when their 2,000 men fell on Cumberland's sleeping 9,000.

Murray gave an order that soldiers should cut the guy ropes of tents and then strike firmly into any bulges which revealed men trapped within, but the opportunity never arose. As men fell by the wayside from hunger, exhaustion or simply deser-tion, it became clear to Lord George that the attack could not take place until daylight. He ordered a halt near Kilravock House, followed by a return to Culloden. This caused an instant quarrel with O'Sullivan and the Prince, and inevitably the retreating Highlanders met the still advancing rearguard in the dark. Charles is reputed to have exclaimed that he had been betrayed (by Lord George). Chaos ensued, but by 6 a.m. the sleepless, exhausted army was back at Culloden House. With no time to pitch tents they were forced to lie on the soaking heather and take what sleep they could. They were a defeated army without yet having met the enemy.

By 9 a.m. on 16 April 1746 Cumberland's well-fed and rested advance guard was at Kilravock House. The duke chided the laird of Kilravock for having met with his cousin Charles Edward earlier that morning. Charles himself had ridden headlong to Inverness to procure supplies for his starving army, and having failed he returned to Culloden House, where he became embroiled in yet another fruitless argument with Lord George, who offered the alternative of a retreat to Inverness, thus drawing Cumberland into an unwinnable siege. Charles would have none of it and insisted on an immediate battle on Drumossie Moor, where the mud-soaked terrain perfectly suited the Hanoverian tactic of fierce attrition by musketry fire and artillery salvoes. Lord George objected to the choice of terrain but was overruled by O'Sullivan and the battle-hungry Prince. The call to arms went out summoning the 2,000 Highlanders still returning from the night march, and it is estimated that a further 1,500 men simply slept through the ensuing battle where fewer than 5,000 Highlanders faced Cumberland's 9,000. The disaster which had been waiting to happen since Derby was about to burst forth.

The two sides would be separated by about two miles of marshland gently sloping upwards to the south, with a hidden swamp in a valley which would nullify any attempt for a screaming charge. To the west was a low wall behind which troops could lie concealed until launching a flank attack. Cumberland sent the Argyll militia to occupy the site, the first example of Scot directly fighting against Scot. Lord George had asked for this wall to be dismantled earlier but he had been ignored. He was now causing discord by according the position of honour on the right of the line to his own Atholl men, instead of the MacDonalds whose place in the battle line this traditionally was and who were now sulkily arriving late on the left.

The Hanoverian artillery had become bogged down in a marsh and would have been susceptible to attack had any Highlanders been prepared. O'Sullivan sent an order to Lord George to attack the static artillery but Lord George refused, being too worried about his Atholl men being outflanked by Campbells behind the wall on the right of the field. By one o'clock the Hanoverian cannon were in place 500 yards from the Highlanders' front line. The artillery consisted of ten three-pounder guns in the front line and other three-pounder guns on a slope behind them. Each gun was fed with one and a half pounds of powder, rammed tight with a wooden plunger, followed by its ball also rammed home, and then the touch hole was fed powder while the gunner shouted 'Ready!' Each gun had a neat pile of already measured powder and a pyramidal pile of cannonballs with water to swab the barrel clean between shots. This was a well-rehearsed drill polished on the fields of Dettingen and Fontenoy, contrasting with the disorganised clansmen desperately trying to learn the art of gunnery with weapons of varying calibre and little ammunition.

The first Hanoverian artillery salvo went over the heads of the front rank but landed among Charles's cavalry including the Fitzjames's Horse and the Lifeguards. These 30 men formed Charles's personal escort. His own horse was struck and he had to dismount and find another, while Captain O'Shea led him to a safer spot albeit without a commanding view of the battlefield. The Highlanders did not, as the Hanoverians did, keep a stock of remounts in the rear.

At first the artillery fired solid shot, which was fatal when a man or horse was struck by it. Even falling short the balls could shatter, and combining with a hail of stones there was an onslaught of deadly effectiveness, immediately piercing huge gaps in the Jacobite line.

After a few salvoes of round-shot the gunners changed to firing 'grape'. For this the guns were loaded not with three-pound cannonballs but with canisters of musket balls, pieces of chain, screws and nails. This grape-shot had a shorter range but turned the air into a hissing maelstrom of death as the flesh-hungry metal pieces tore into everything.

The ground seemed to tremble with the roar of the artillery and the sky was blotted out with the acrid smoke of the black powder. The gentle southerly breeze blew the smoke, with the rain, into the faces of the clansmen so that they could no longer see the enemy who was scything down their line. Their few musket-bearers were forced to fire at an invisible enemy too far distant to be harmed. After nine minutes of firing the Jacobite guns fell silent, while the hapless clansmen stood impotently in the rain to receive the next artillery salvoes. Charles had given an order to the desperate Highlanders to charge, but the officers carrying the command were hit by musket fire and the men had to continue obediently standing in line while being slaughtered by the dozen. The hideously wounded lay screaming where they fell while the survivors closed the ranks, providing a greater target for the artillery.

Cumberland was well pleased with the carnage his guns had caused without any serious damage to his own forces, and his infantry, who had been tensely awaiting the feared screaming charge of the Highlanders, relaxed for a moment with their coats over the barrels of their muskets to ensure dry powder when the time for their volleys came.

The clansmen were desperate to charge, not only to escape the unfamiliar and deadly onslaught of the artillery, but also to engage in the hand-to-hand fighting at which they excelled. They would also be fighting fellow Scots whom they considered as traitors. Cumberland's force included the Royal Scots, the King's Own Scottish Borderers, the Royal Scots Fusiliers, the Border Regiment and the Argyll Militia, while Charles's army had 300 Irish Picquets and 350 men from the Garde Ecossaise (Scots mercenaries in the service of Louis XV), so the misconception that Culloden was Scots versus English can be easily discounted.

Battalion commanders were glancing behind them for a signal from the Prince, who had remounted and was now surrounded by Lifeguards, further from the front line. But when the order finally came, the ground was thoroughly sodden and the charge had to be made with frozen bare feet ploughing through glutinous bogs. Then, with drawn claymores, having thrown away their now soaking and unfamiliar muskets and with their plaids hitched thigh-high, they advanced towards an enemy they could not see, still hidden by the smoke of cannon fire. The Hanoverian infantry lines, in the regular ranks they had formed at Fontenoy and elsewhere in the Netherlands, clad in scarlet coats and black tricorne hats, stood tall in dry white knee-length gaiters over leather boots with their newly bayoneted muskets at the ready. They were three deep, with the front rank kneeling. When this rank fired they immediately withdrew to the rear and their places were taken by the second-rank men who fired as the front rank reloaded in the rear. Then the third rank completed the manoeuvre to make way for the now reloaded front men to retake their places, as the onslaught was repeated over and over again. This rolling volley meant that the clansmen were charging blind into almost continuous fire. Until the machine guns of the First World War there was no deadlier enemy than disciplined infantry.

At two feet from the Hanoverians the Highlanders came out of the smoke to meet the glittering line of bayonets. It was said that if grape were the king of battles the queen was the bayonet. The front rank hoisted their muskets shoulder-high and waited for the Highlanders to impale themselves. Against infantry seasoned on the fields of Europe the frontal charge was a suicide attack, and Clan Chattan bore the brunt of the slaughter. Before they had reached within 20 yards of the Hanoverian line 300 clansmen and 19 out of 21 officers were dead. The second line of clansmen had to advance over the bodies of their dead and wounded comrades.

Lord George was doing no better on the right of the line. His Atholl men charged up the hill, but the Campbells of the Argyll Militia poured flanking fire into them. Less than half the Highlanders reached the bayonets of Cumberland's infantry. The charge was halted, and cavalry under Brevet-Major James Wolfe charged among them. Highlanders had an instinctive fear of charging cavalry, and unlike Falkirk, when they charged downhill into the panicking horses, here they had to receive the charge themselves. They were either shot from the right by the Campbells or sabred into butcher's meat by Wolfe's men. Wolfe was amazed at their determination against all odds, but eventually the charge halted and they fell to the blood-sodden heather. Perhaps what he witnessed in the rain on Drumossie Moor came back to him in 1759 on the Heights of Abraham, when he led the attack with Highland soldiers saying, 'If they are lost 'tis no great matter.' However, he behaved in an otherwise civilised manner at Culloden, later refusing Hawley's instruction to shoot a helpless wounded Highlander.

To the left of Lord George was Cameron of Lochiel. His men attempted a charge, but while Lochiel was drawing his sword he had both ankles shattered by grapeshot. The Cameron clansmen met the death-dealing volleys from kneeling Hanoverians who had leisure to pick their targets. Lochiel was carried by four clansmen to a cottage which was later searched by Cumberland's men, although they missed the chief, who had been taken to Cluny Macpherson's home in Badenoch. After unsuccessfully attempting a reassembly of forces Lochiel managed to escape to France where he took command of the Albany regiment. He died and was buried in Bergues near Dunkirk.

All across the field the Highlanders were either losing a hand-to-hand fight of bayonet against claymore, or were starting to fall back. As always a practical observer of the inevitable, Lord George left the moor with a regiment for Ruthven, where he hoped to organise a resistance, but he received a sharp letter from Charles Edward dismissing him from his command. Lord George replied vituperatively and in equally bad spirits, rebuking the Prince for slavishly following bad advice. Fleeing to Europe, Lord George was well received in Rome by Charles's father who granted him a pension. He travelled variously in the Netherlands and was buried in Medemblik in 1760. His grave is still visited by latter-day Jacobites and some of them decorate it with heather plucked at Culloden.

The Prince himself, who had been contemplating a counter-attack which, with his remnant of thoroughly demoralised troops, would have added a massacre to the ongoing slaughter, was led off the field, against his will and in tears, by O'Sullivan taking his bridle. O'Shea, the commander of his Lifeguards, is reputed to have shouted after him, 'Run, you Italian coward!' Two unnecessary and erroneous insults.

There was no counter-charge by the Hanoverians, as the gunners swabbed their over-heated cannon and the infantry leant on their muskets. One Scots fusilier, a veteran of European wars, commented, 'I never saw a field thicker of dead.' In less than an hour on the afternoon of 16 April 1746 the Forty-Five was finished and the legends began.

Often after such a battle there is an eerie quiet on the field, but this was not the case on Drumossie Moor, since there were so many wounded either from bayonet thrusts or from musket or artillery fire now lying screaming in untreated agony. This was brought to an end by Hawley, who rode on to the field with his dragoons and urged his men to slaughter the wounded. This they did either by lance, if the unfortunate man was lying on the ground, or by a sabre blow to the neck, if he was standing or running away. Hawley may well have been taking a savage revenge for his defeat at Falkirk, but he could certainly share in the epithet of 'Butcher' levelled at Cumberland, more for his actions after Culloden than for his behaviour during the battle. He became a favourite of Cumberland and commanded his cavalry in 1747 when they were defeated by Marshal Saxe at Lauffeldt. He was consoled with the governorship of Portsmouth where he died peacefully in 1759. His tombstone at Hartley Wintney in Hampshire does not mention Culloden.

There is no evidence that Cumberland himself gave the order to take no prisoners, but he certainly did nothing to stop the ensuing massacre. There is a disputed account that a written order was found on a dead Jacobite officer commanding that no prisoners were to be taken. It is unsigned and probably a forgery.

Figures are impossible to verify, but it seems that during the 45-minute battle about 50 of Cumberland's 8,000 men were killed, as opposed to the Jacobite losses of 1,000 killed on the battlefield and 1,500 in the aftermath. The slaughter of the wounded was an action taken to ensure that such a rising could never recur.

Finally, a Major Kennedy rode to the Prince, who was now at a safe distance, and begged him to leave the field altogether. After some persuasion and in a half-dazed state the Prince was escorted by O'Sullivan, Lord Elcho and others to Strathair, about 19 miles south of Culloden where he stayed for the night at Gortlick House. There he renewed his acquaintance with the ever-changing Lord Lovat.

At Gortlick House an argument raged between rallying the 1,500 men, remnants of the army at Ruthven where Lord George had hoped for a rendezvous, or undertaking long-term guerrilla warfare in the Highlands. Needless to say, the Jacobites had made no future plans in the event of defeat, and confusion had resulted from Lord George's vituperative letter. In the end Charles gave a verbal message, to be carried to the survivors at Ruthven, that every man should seek his safety in the best way he could.

The lucky few fled the field. One man, the Chevalier Johnstone, fled as far as Edinburgh where he still felt himself so much a fugitive that he hid under a haystack at Lady Janet Douglas's farm at Drumsheugh, on what is now the site of St Mary's Cathedral of the Scottish Episcopal Church. The mood of the capital gave him reason to be afraid, since within sight of Hawley's gibbets the mob burned the houses of Catholics, and the General Assembly of the Church of Scotland offered prayers for the Duke of Cumberland, whose 'illustrious name, so dear to us' might 'share the happiness and glory bestowed by divine mercy'. A special edition of the newspaper giving thanks for Scotland's deliverance from Catholicism at Culloden was printed.

For the Prince himself, with a price of £30,000 on his head alive or dead, there must have been a sense of inevitability that he would be captured. If that was the case then there was never any actual sign of it. But there would be no mercy for the fugitive Prince.

Chapter 9

After Culloden Prince Charles saved his own skin, fled with his mistress Flora MacDonald and left the clans to the mercy of 'Butcher' Cumberland

An affair, whether of the heart or simply from the human need for companionship, was the furthest thing from the Prince's mind in late April 1746. He was well aware that Cumberland meant to eradicate all support for the Jacobite cause by the most stringent of methods, including the capture and possible execution of all supporters of the Prince, as well as Charles himself. His most urgent need now was for escape.

Cumberland took possession first of Culloden House, Charles's recently vacated headquarters, and then of Inverness, where the bridge had been held by Lord Lovat who, wisely and habitually, had an immediate change of heart and switched his already fragile loyalty to the Government side. This deed profited him not at all, since in March 1747 he was tried for treason and became the last person in Britain to be publicly beheaded. Cumberland set up his headquarters in the house of the dowager Lady Mackintosh, recently the hostess of Charles, and had Colonel Anne brought to him as a Jacobite prisoner. She was, in fact, treated with all civility and released.

He also sent a party of soldiers to search for rebels and to note that no quarter was to be given. This was the start of what would develop, almost of its own momentum, into the destruction of the Highlands. But before setting out on the well nigh impossible task of scouring the Highlands for one fugitive, no matter how important, Cumberland first turned his attention to the Jacobite prisoners.

Culloden had been a distinctive battle for two reasons. First, since the Highland forces had largely been assembled by feudal obligations, it was the last battle on British soil fought by a feudal army, and second, thanks to the savage ministrations of Hawley and Cumberland, there were no captive wounded to speak of. But there were prisoners, at present being held in the Tolbooth jail in Inverness which had been occupied by the Hanoverian army. To the soldiers the town was a far cry from the garrison towns of the Low Countries with their multiplicity of taverns and brothels which had seen armies come and go for many years. Inverness was a market town for the impoverished Highlands which, according to a contemporary historian, in 1746 boasted only five citizens who owned a hat. They were the provost, the sheriff and the three ministers, which allows us to reflect on an inaccurate but telling demographic survey of the town.

The Tolbooth jail held 36 deserters from Cumberland's army. Every morning a dismal squad of these men walked a mile to the gallows, each bearing a card with his offence written on it. Then they were stripped naked and hanged. The exception was one Ninian Dunbar, who had not only deserted but also stolen the gold and scarlet officer's coat of Major Lockhart. Hawley was amused by the hanging of a man dressed as an officer. After half an hour he was cut down and stripped, and his naked corpse was then rehoisted and left to hang. Lockhart got his coat back and Hawley had had his macabre joke.

No sooner had Hawley emptied the Tolbooth of deserters than it began to fill up with Jacobite prisoners. Many of these men – and a few women – had taken no part in the battle but were rounded up by marauding dragoons. Churches, stables and barns were used as makeshift jails with no sanitation and little in the way of food, since the Hanoverian army was happily consuming the supplies which should have gone to Charles's army before the battle. Death and disease were rampant, a situation exacerbated by the Privy Council's decision in May that no trials should take place in Scotland. Prison hulks were sent to the Moray Firth, and captives were loaded on prior to their journey to the Thames, where they were held indefinitely on board prison ships. One witness tells of no fewer than 400 men dying on the hulks opposite Tilbury. The survivors were eventually transported to the colonies – either to the brutal labour gangs in Australia or to the fever-infested plantations in Barbados. So great was the inefficiency of the system that many prisoners escaped to return to their glens, but over 1,000 died of one sort or another of indefinite exile.

Last-minute confessions by prisoners give a handy snapshot of motives and ambitions. Thomas Sydal, about to be executed on Kennington Green, declared himself a member of a pure Episcopal Church and prayed for the restoration of the Stuarts who, curiously, were bitter opponents of Episcopalianism, while Donald MacDonell declared himself an unworthy member of the Roman Catholic Church and hoped 'to free this unhappy island from usurpation, corruption, treachery and bribery'. Lord Balmerino, before he was beheaded on 18 August 1746 at the Tower of London, gives us a picture of an anti-revolutionary aristocrat, who when Charles came to Edinburgh might have been excused from active service by reason of his age, but out of 'bounden and indispensible duty' joined the Prince. He tells us of Charles's incomparable sweetness, his affability, his compassion, his justice, his temperance, his patience and his courage which 'were virtues seldom all to be found in one man'. Fortunately, Balmerino did not live to see Charles betray almost all these attributes.

Meanwhile Cumberland received inaccurate news that Lochiel was raising a retaliatory force and was about to link up with the vanished Prince, and he began to reinforce the Highland forts. Inverness was already garrisoned and he sent men to Fort William and Fort Augustus. Orders were given that any Highlander still bearing arms was to be arrested, and on giving them up would be allowed to return to his home – an order impossible to enforce on a people who carried arms as part of normal dress. Cumberland was attempting to put out a heath fire covering thousands of acres simply by stamping on patches of it.

Immediately after the conclusion of hostilities on Drumossie Moor on 26 April, Charles, with an escort of O'Sullivan, Father Allan Macdonald, a Catholic chaplain, and Edward Bourk, or

Burke, a sedan-chair porter from Edinburgh but a local man now acting as a guide, travelled to Invergarry, arriving at the castle in the small hours of 17 May. They left on the same day for Loch Lochy and Loch Arkaig, having skirted Fort Augustus and turned west before reaching Fort William. On the shores of Loch Arkaig they were accommodated in the cottage of a local man, and the Prince had his first full night's sleep since the eve of Culloden.

In a later memoir Bourk gave a picture of the Prince's conditions: 'The many wants he suffered, the badly dressed diets, the many bad beds he lay in, the many cold and wet beds in the open fields, all of which he cheerfully and patiently put up with.' He had ridden over 50 miles, often in the dark and probably in the clothes he had worn in the battle, where he would have been drenched by the rain. His fresh clothes and personal goods were still in Culloden Castle, never to be retrieved. Any man would have been in a state of exhaustion, while the Prince was still recuperating from influenza and scarlet fever. Gone was the finery of satin and velvet, the stars of chivalry and the finely dressed wigs. The Prince now had to make do with what was left of the clothes he had chosen for the battle, and with no chance of replacements his stockings and shirts would have to be washed, worn and mended as became possible. His diet would be that of his hosts – usually fish and oatcakes – washed down with water or whisky. The Prince gained respect for drinking Scotch whisky, as opposed to the French brandy he was accustomed to, but this was a matter of expediency not diplomacy.

Charles now had to abandon his horse since the way became too rough, and he continued on foot. By night he travelled south to Loch nan Uamh, where he was lodged by the sometime surgeon of Glengarry's regiment in a cottage in Glenbeasdale. He was so tired that he could neither eat nor drink and he had to be helped to a straw bed on which he rested for five days. This cottage was near to where he had landed nearly ten months previously.

On 30 April two French warships came into sight. They were the *Mars* and the *Bellone*, bringing 40,000 louis d'or and fresh supplies. They were unshipped successfully, which greatly heartened the Jacobites who had started to reassemble around the Prince. But also arriving were the *Greyhound*, *Baltimore* and *Terror*, sloops of the Royal Navy, and after a six-hour sea battle the severely damaged French ships fled back south to return to France. The treasure was hastily buried as secretly as possible by the shores of Loch Arkaig. Now, with a greater war chest than previously, word was sent out to the chiefs to meet at Invermaillie on 8 May, but only about 600 men answered the call. The fresh call to arms was a failure, and Charles's plight worsened when Cumberland reinforced the Highland forts and started punitive expeditions into the glens searching for him, or at least for what information could be gathered. But there was no intelligence to be gained, even under torture. Charles was now a fugitive in the Outer Hebrides.

Meanwhile on the mainland, Cumberland was still nervous at the prospect of a fresh rising and he increased his punitive measures. He had asked the Duke of Newcastle for guidance and was assured that 'as a general of His Majesty's army your Royal Highness has his [Newcastle's] authority to do whatever is necessary for the suppression of this unnatural rebellion'.

With this *carte blanche*, Cumberland was determined 'to bruise those bad seeds spread about this country so as they may never shoot again'.

He despatched Major (soon to be Brigadier) John Mordaunt with 900 men to raid the Fraser country at the head of the Beauly Firth, a few miles west of Inverness. Mordaunt could be sure that he had great latitude in carrying out his orders to disarm any people found carrying weapons and arrest any who had taken part in the rising. However, Mordaunt was discriminating in his looting, bringing back 1,000 bottles of Madeira and claret to be sold off among the soldiery, a library said to be worth £400, as well as quantities of malt, oatmeal and salmon. When their carts were loaded to the brim, the remainder of the loot was burnt, as well as the cottages, beds and personal possessions of the cottagers. Since no prisoners were brought back we must suppose that the men resisted arrest and were killed. This action set the pattern for the rest of Cumberland's subjection of the Highlands, in which not only Highlanders suffered. An expedition to Aberdeen saw Catholic and Episcopalian meeting houses destroyed. A Scot of noble ancestry, Captain Grant of Knockando and Strathspey, took 200 men of Loudoun's regiment into Lochaber, killed the men, stripped and raped the women and left the children to starve, naked, on the moors. Even allowing for the hyperbole of horror in which the stereotypical report is that all women are raped, all houses destroyed and children left to starve, the depredations that were visited on a peasant population, many of whom could have had neither involvement in, nor concept of, the conflict, were savage events and leave a permanent stain on the record of British soldiery.

Cumberland's hand was strengthened with the activities of the Royal Navy on the east coast. Their ships harried the coastal villages, burning and looting as well as taking prisoners, who could be sold into indentured servitude with the merchant ships' captains, who would then sell on the unfortunates to plantation owners in the colonies. This system had already been practised by some clan chiefs, who found that they could make more money from their land by farming it themselves and had sold their tacksmen into this form of virtual slavery. The tacksmen had no way of complaining about the activities of their feudal superior, and these early 'clearances' went largely unnoticed. The much-vaunted clan system had been starting to break down long before the arrival of Prince Charles. Cumberland and Culloden merely gave it another push over the edge.

Too often the atrocities after Culloden have been blamed on an English hatred of the Scots, but Scottish Lowlanders also took part. The short-tempered Major Lockhart led a raiding party into Glenmoriston, notwithstanding the fact that the glen had already been emptied of weapons. Almost as routine, all the men were shot, their wives and daughters raped, their houses burned and their cattle seized. He then meted out the same punishment to the Chisholms of Strathglass. These raids were only two of many, and much happened more casually. One soldier wrote home that while on patrol his officer had let them take a break beside a stream, and then, in the afternoon, they 'shot some Scotchmen for sport'.

By early summer Cumberland was feeling secure enough to move his headquarters, and on 23 May 1746 the army moved to what was left of Fort Augustus. This garrison had to be fed, and wholesale cattle-thieving took place under the excuse of provisioning. On one raid the indefatigable Major Lockhart netted almost £50. Other raids merely found burnt cottages and, occasionally, the emaciated bodies of women and children who had died of starvation and exposure. That many more cattle than were needed were taken can be seen by the fact that Fort Augustus became a celebrated cattle-dealing centre. Army officers encouraged visits from southern dealers to purchase their loot, while beyond the confines of the camp the clansmen and their families were starving.

A report from the fort stated:

> While our army stayed here we had near twenty thousand head of cattle brought in, such as oxen, horses, sheep and goats taken from the rebels (whose houses we also frequently plundered and burnt) by parties sent out for them, and in search of the Pretender, so that great numbers of our men grew rich in their shares of the spoil.

But the search for the Pretender was getting nowhere. With a price of £30,000 on his head – unlike the £5 General Huske offered for every rebel's head brought to him, an offer that was not accepted – and the number of people who must have had a sighting of him, it was amazing that no information was forthcoming. Amazing, but not that surprising since the Prince was no longer on the mainland of Scotland.

On the evening of 26 April Charles set sail from Loch nan Uamh with Donald MacLeod, a 70-year-old Skye fisherman. Charles had initially wanted to sail for Skye and ask for help to contact France from either MacDonald of Sleat or Macleod of Macleod, but he was warned that either man would immediately turn Charles in to Cumberland and claim the reward. For once in his life Charles listened to good advice and was also dissuaded from sailing to Eriskay, where he would have run into three sloops of the Royal Navy which were patrolling the islands. The navy had even sailed as far as the remote settlement of St Kilda, finding only baffled islanders who had never heard of Jacobites or Hanoverians. Charles was persuaded to seek help on the 'Long Island' – Lewis in the Outer Hebrides – and they set sail. Almost immediately an easterly gale arose, but thanks to Macleod's seamanship they managed to make landfall on Benbecula, albeit with a shattered bowsprit and a severely seasick Prince.

For two days the fugitives stayed in a deserted and half-ruined hut with a turf roof, being looked after by the aged Ranald MacDonald, an old chief of Clanranald whose son had led the clan at Culloden. The old man had no difficulty in putting his duty towards his Prince before the dizzying sum of the reward. In any case cash was largely an unknown commodity to the lower level of Highlanders, who dealt by barter in a subsistence economy.

Charles's scheme was still to sail northwards for Lewis, where he might find passage to Orkney and then on to Norway. For some reason the idea of escaping to France had, for the moment, left him. Making landfall on Scalpay, a tiny island to the south of Lewis, they were sheltered by Donald Campbell, the sole inhabitant, who managed to procure some food. Suddenly militiamen landed, but the party managed to escape. Now they would pose as a group of shipwrecked Orcadians with Charles as Mr Sinclair and O'Sullivan as his father. They eventually came ashore at the head of Loch Seaforth, and, after an 18-hour hike across the peat bog with an incompetent guide, they reached the hamlet of Arnish to the south of Stornoway at 11 a.m. on 5 May, only to find that the town knew of their coming and was ready to betray them. The small party spent four days and nights in an abandoned hut on the uninhabited Eilean Lubbard, from where they could see the sea crowded with the various naval ships sent to find them.

Charles was in a dreadful condition. His silk stockings had long since been shredded by heather and gorse, and his legs were a network of unhealed scratches. His pale complexion had become sunburned and his red-gold hair bleached. His skin was now a mass of painful blotches inflicted by the savage attentions of the West Highland midge for whom a sweating fair skin was an irresistible feast. Charles had never shaved himself in his life, and now that he had no barber a straggly, unkempt beard covered his face. He wore a borrowed brown coat and his blistered feet were shod in a pair of ill-fitting brogues. He was no longer 'Bonnie'.

On 10 May they sailed south again, avoiding naval patrols and being unable to land for fear of searching militias, until they were directed to a safe refuge at Corrodale on the east coast of South Uist. Here they were lodged in a cottage with all the comforts that could be hoped for, and the Prince's spirits lifted. He was able to bathe, and to rest on a comfortable bed with fresh linen. He could hunt and fish. During this period, two French sloops, the *Bellone* and *Mars*, landed at Loch nan Uamh with 40,000 louis d'or and fresh supplies, but before unloading was complete they had been driven off by the arrival of the Royal Navy. They were forced to flee for France, carrying with them, among others, the Duke of Perth, who died on the voyage, and Lord Elcho who made it into exile with the other Jacobite refugees.

Charles, meanwhile, was starting to exhibit one of the traits that would be his tragedy in later life. Eschewing the native whisky for his favoured brandy, he was drinking prodigious amounts – up to a bottle a day according to one account.

News that Cumberland's net was tightening around them caused a return to the 'Long Island', where they expected help from MacDonald of Boisdale. Unfortunately he had been captured, and there now followed days of horror as they were forced to hide in caves and sleep with no cover except for the rain-sodden sails. However, they were contacted by Hugh MacDonald who, although he commanded the militia in South Uist, was a Jacobite sympathiser. He suggested a meeting with his stepdaughter, Flora MacDonald.

She was 24 years old and the daughter of Ranald Mac-Donald, who had died when she was a child. Her mother was abducted and forced into a remarriage. Flora was then cared for by the clan chief, Hugh MacDonald, who saw to her education in Edinburgh as a Presbyterian. With the cool logic of one trained in the Edinburgh of the Enlightenment, she was, at first, hostile to the plan O'Sullivan put to her, that she should travel to Skye with the Prince disguised as her maidservant, but Charles's Stuart charm won her round. Though she carried out her part of the scheme with courage and brisk efficiency, it seems that she was cautious of any emotional involvement with Charles, and the idea of the two as lovers clinging to each other as they hid in the heather is totally absurd.

Flora at once set out to arrange for suitable clothes for her new 'maidservant', and was promptly arrested by a government patrol who took her to their commander. Since the commander in question was her clan chief and *de facto* father, she explained the plot, and he arranged passports for the journey of herself and an Irish girl, 'Betty Burke', whom his wife would 'find useful as spinster'.

Having spent the night sheltering unsuccessfully under a rock, and waited impatiently all the next day, Charles finally reached a rendezvous on Loch Uskavagh. Here he dismissed John O'Sullivan, who had given him so much bad advice, on the dubious grounds that since he could not speak Gaelic he could not pose as a servant of Flora's. He was shortly taken prisoner but would later reappear in Charles's story.

The Prince was now dressed in a quilted petticoat, a sprigged calico gown, shoes, stockings and a wig and hood. He wore a ribbon on his head, which was later kept by a lady as a souvenir.

> Most honoured riband, of all else take place
> Of greens and blues and all their tawdry race
> Thou wast the laurel the fair temple bound
> Of Royal Charles, for greatness so renowned
> This I'll reserve, as heaven reserve his crown
> Till his rebellious foes be overthrown
> Then in thy place a diadem shall shine
> His by his virtues, as by right divine.

Charles wanted to carry a pistol but Flora forbade it, since if he was searched its presence would reveal his imposture as a

Highland maidservant. Charles replied that a pistol was not all that such a search would discover. There is no record of whether Flora was amused.

They sailed as it grew dark on 27 June and reached Vaternish Point on Skye the next morning, where they came under fire from a mixture of militiaman and Macleod clansmen. After a brief chase they made a safe landfall at Trotternish. They then travelled to Kilbride House to meet Lady MacDonald of Sleat, with Flora, as became her station, on a horse and her dishevelled 'maidservant' loping along clumsily behind her. Any close examination of his disguise would have fooled nobody, and at one point they narrowly avoided discovery by a party returning from church who were diverted by Charles's clumsiness in handling his petticoats while crossing a ford. They were always a hair's breadth – literally a beard's hair breadth – away from capture.

Since Charles's unaccustomed footwear prevented him from keeping up, Flora went on alone to forewarn Lady MacDonald of Sleat, but on arriving at the house Flora was horrified to see two military horses with an attendant trooper at the door. Lady MacDonald was entertaining a lieutenant of Cumberland's army, unaware that the prospect of a £30,000 reward was mincing ever closer in unfamiliar shoes on the beach nearby. Flora diverted the officer and sent a note arranging that Charles should spend the night at the house of MacDonald of Kingsburgh, Lady MacDonald's factor. Kingsburgh's wife, who, on seeing the bizarre spectacle of Betty Burke, demanded to know who was the 'old muckle trollop', then alarmed everyone by reaching forward and feeling the stubble of the Prince's chin.

When she was told who he was, the astonished hostess fell to her knees, and Charles was entertained with as much luxury as an estate factor could provide. Charles provided a lock of his hair for his erstwhile hosts, and Mrs MacDonald showed him how a lady kept her snuff in her muff.

This advice was unnecessary, since next morning he changed back into men's clothing. Flora had ridden ahead to Portree and arranged for the Prince to cross to the neighbouring island of Raasay. Here Charles saw first-hand the effects of Cumberland's depredations. Raasay had once had over 300 cottages and now there were none. All had been burned, the men slaughtered and the women of all ages raped indiscriminately. A Whig writer tells us that in Knoydart even the shellfish were wantonly destroyed, and even if this is a hyperbolic metaphor the sentiment engendered by Cumberland's policy of destruction is startlingly clear.

The Prince was quartered in a hut so low that he could not stand up, and was forced to attempt sleep without blankets or bedding on the bare earth. That night he bade farewell to Flora, hoping that 'they would meet one day in St James's'. He thus demonstrated that his ambition was still to rule from London and not from Edinburgh. On his father's death he intended to be Charles III of Great Britain. Scotland was a mere stepping-stone.

Charles and Flora had been together for only four days, during most of which time she had preceded the Prince to make arrangements for his onward passage. The episode demonstrates how Charles could, by often wrong-headed determination, turn simple events into dangerous adventures, and how memory can turn dangerous adventures into romances. After all, Napoleon once said, 'History is a fable agreed upon.'

Flora's adventurous life continued, with her arrest shortly after Charles's flight to Raasay. She was imprisoned in the Tower of London, although she was allowed to lodge outside the actual tower. Released, like other Jacobite prisoners, after the Act of Indemnity of 1747, a somewhat grudging act with over 80 exceptions, she married Captain Allan MacDonald and the couple emigrated to North Carolina to support King George III's forces. Returning in 1779, she was wounded when her ship was attacked by a privateer. She finally settled in Kingsburgh where, as the mother of a large family, she died in 1790 aged 68.

Realising that Raasay offered no hiding places, on 1 July Charles crossed back to Skye, then returned to Mallaig on the mainland three days later. For the next two months the Prince's life was one of narrow escapes, hearing about his sometime helpers being arrested, and sleeping in caves and improvised shelters. Then on 29 August Charles was united with Lochiel's son (the old man still being too crippled to travel), who found the Prince barefoot, in an old black kilt and a dirty shirt, and with a long red beard. This last is puzzling, since only two months had passed since the Prince was in female dress. Did he wear a kerchief over the lower half of his face? Or did he grow a long beard in two months? Both seem unlikely. Perhaps 'unshaven' has grown in the telling.

He now habitually carried a gun, with a pistol and dirk on his belt. In spite of his unkempt appearance it was a very hearty reunion, with plenty of food and, of course, industrial quantities of whisky. On 1 September they were joined by Cluny Macpherson and after three more nights of reminiscing and drinking the Prince moved with Cluny to 'Cluny's Cage'. This was the epitome of an outlaw's hideout, on the southern slope of Ben Alder and overlooking the 12-mile stretch of Loch Ericht. It was divided into separate rooms, including a kitchen, although a system of heather baffles dispersed the cooking smoke. An efficient system of sentries and its commanding position meant that it was invulnerable to surprise. It also had a well-organised supply chain for food and drink, although there was a permanent spring nearby. Cluny lived here in safety and luxury for nearly ten years.

The Prince stayed here for the next eight days, meeting other renegades including Lochgarry, who had recommended setting an ambush to assassinate Cumberland after Culloden. The Prince had overruled him on the grounds that he was not a murderer. On this occasion Lochgarry promised the support of 5,000 men for a revival of the rising. Charles was immediately enthusiastic about this, but was wisely advised against it by Cluny and young Lochiel until, on 12 September, he heard the news he had been waiting for. Two French privateers, manned by Irishmen with Jacobite sympathies and sailing with the full authority of Louis XV, had arrived at Loch nan Uamh. They were safely moored, and a convenient gale kept the Royal Navy occupied elsewhere. Charles left Cluny on 13 September, and barely a week later, by 19 September, he was on board. The escapees had travelled by day and night, with Charles quite unnecessarily changing into women's clothes by day. He boarded the *L'Heureux* with 23 gentlemen and 107 men of common rank. Before sailing,

Charles sent sums of money to those who had helped him. He would never see Scotland again.

He had been at large as the most sought-after fugitive in Britain for five months, from 16 April until 19 September, with a reward of £30,000 for his capture. He had met countless people of all classes, and nobody had even attempted to betray his whereabouts. Not all of them were adherents to the Jacobite cause but all would have been aware of his identity.

The London Government had already moved to prevent any recurrence of the rising by passing the Disarming Act in August 1746. This required Highlanders to swear that they would never possess a gun, sword, pistol or any weapon whatsoever, and would never wear tartan, plaid or any part of the Highland garb. The clauses referring to dress were repealed in 1782, and the Highland regiments, proud in tartan and armed to the teeth, became the enforcers of the British Empire.

Possibly more important was the Heritable Jurisdiction Act of 1746, which removed the power of the clan chiefs – the so-called power of 'pit and gallows' – and meant that clansmen were now simply tenants who shared the chief's name. Since many chiefs had already abandoned the system of tacksmen and replaced them with tenant farmers who provided a more reliable income, the decline of the clans cannot be laid wholly at Cumberland's door. Some chiefs on the west coast had discovered that selling their clansmen to merchant ships' captains heading across the Atlantic brought in more profit than collecting unreliable rents. Thus the decay of the old semi-feudal system was well under way before the rising in 1745.

Chapter 10

Charles Edward was a promiscuous libertine and died a hopeless drunk

On the morning of 30 September 1746 Prince Charles was on board the *L'Heureux* heading for Nantes on the north-west coast of France, but for some unexplained reason the captain changed his mind and steered instead for Roscoff on the Channel coast. If he had continued on his original course he would have met with a Royal Navy squadron under General St Clair, which was en route to Quiberon Bay to launch a surprise attack. As well as being taken prisoner, Charles would have come across the general's secretary, David Hume. The two men would meet two years later under equally bizarre circumstances.

Charles was now the most famous man in Europe, having tweaked the nose of the King of Britain and, in spite of the awful cost of Culloden, got away with it. Now he was welcomed back in France and on 17 October he was reunited with his brother Henry. While savouring the adulation of the crowd he failed to spot his brother, who lunged forward to greet him. Mistaking this for an assassination attempt, one of Charles's

Highlander bodyguards drew his claymore and stepped in front of the Prince, but Charles intervened in time and a joyful reunion took place. After a private audience with Louis and his family, the brothers were entertained by most of the French aristocracy, culminating on 23 October with a state dinner at Fontainebleau attended by the king himself. Charles's entourage consisted of three carriages with ten running footmen. He wore a coat of rose-coloured velvet over a waistcoat of gold brocade. His cockade and shoe buckles were decorated with diamonds and he glittered like the star he was, as opposed to the ragged fugitive sheltering in dripping caves. Also present was the most famous woman in Europe, the Marquise de Pompadour, better known as Madame de Pompadour, who had been Louis's mistress since 1745. A scandal had arisen when Louis took a commoner as his *maîtresse en titre*, even though she was married to Charles-Guillaume d'Étioles, a minor nobleman. Prince Charles, whose mother was a relative of Louis's queen, Marie Leszcinska, was now being treated as a member of Louis's most private circle, and the king promised to give Charles accommodation at the royal palace at Vincennes. At the reception Charles would have met the Duc de Bouillon, married to Charles's aunt, and the two men struck up a lifelong friendship.

Temporarily the brothers set up court at Henry's house at Clichy, with Lochiel once more at Charles's side. Also still with the Prince was George Kelly, a Church of England parson who had joined Jacobitism in the 1715 rising and had been part of Charles's inner household since his childhood in the Palazzo Muti. He wielded considerable power as one of the Seven Men of Moidart.

With the knowledge that Charles had the favour of Louis, the French nobility flocked to Clichy to ally themselves with the 'gay chevalier', and he ensured his popularity by attending the opera on 28 October. He had last attended the Paris opera in February 1745 with an ineffective incognito, but now he could appear as a Stuart prince. The audience rose, cheering and applauding, when he entered and he had to remain after the performance to take bow after bow – more, in fact, than those received by the cast. This was much more to his taste than being welcomed by a single crofter on Benbecula.

A regular visitor to Clichy was the Duc de Richelieu, whose army had so nearly embarked in support while Charles was at Derby. The relationship was not altogether easy since the profligate duke loathed Henry's extreme piety. Henry would rise at 6 a.m., pray for an hour, then eat a meagre breakfast before spending another hour with his confessor, and the rest of the day in his chapel praying or hearing repeated masses. He was also rumoured to be a closet homosexual. No doubt the politically minded Richelieu realised that Charles's new-found popularity with the Paris crowds would lessen his favour with the court. Louis was presently taking part in discussions at Breda which would form the basis for the treaty of Aix-la-Chapelle, by which he would agree to exile Charles from France.

In the interim Louis sent a minor civil servant to inform Charles that he could have temporary use of a house at Bercy plus a less-than-princely monthly allowance of 12,000 livres. Charles was apoplectic with rage. Not only were the promises made at Fontainebleau ignored, but also the offer was parsimonious in the extreme and made by a junior official.

Charles interpreted this as a gross snub and as always when his expectations were unsatisfied, he fell into a fever and retired to bed, arising to accuse his brother of having alienated Richelieu with his pious behaviour. Also an old enmity between Kelly and Lochiel, which had lasted since Moidart, surfaced violently and Lochiel left the Prince's service. The old Cameron warrior had been, after Lord George Murray, one of the father figures that Charles had lacked all his life, and the downward spiral of his life was now beginning.

Charles made repeated entreaties to Louis XV for support, only to have his requests ignored. He sublimated his unhappiness in lavish entertaining, spending over 20,000 livres in one month when the monthly allowance had been reduced to 12,000 livres for both brothers. Encouraged by Kelly, he entertained prostitutes by the legion. Kelly, on one demented occasion, even suggested to Henry that he might help in procuring new girls. The situation could not continue and the two men moved into separate but adjacent houses in Paris. Charles accepted, but did not use, his pension from Louis, since he still wanted to demonstrate his freedom from French influence, depending instead on contributions from Jacobite supporters in Britain and lavish credit from Waters, his bankers in Paris.

The air was thick with plot and counter-plot. Charles was unaware that his father was encouraging Henry to campaign for a cardinal's hat. Henry was plotting to visit Spain to raise support for his brother. Louis was agreeing to everything with no intention of doing anything. Charles toyed with the idea of forestalling Henry with a visit to Spain himself, ignoring the fact that leaving France, where he was a guest of the king, without a royal *congé* was a direct insult. Finally, he chose the worst option. On 25 January 1747 he left for Avignon, virtually a papal island surrounded by French territory. He assured all his baffled supporters that Avignon was a staging post for his visit to Spain, and he sent letters to the king and queen ahead of him. He was granted a very formal audience, with all the empty promises expected of a Catholic sovereign, and was referred to the chief minister, Carvajal, who gave no definite support but promised to defray Charles's expenses. He also met the castrato Farinelli, who had been introduced to the Prince previously in Italy, and who on this occasion presumed on previous acquaintance and shook Charles's hand unbidden. Such informality may have been acceptable under a wet rock in Lochaber, but in the Spanish court it resulted in Charles cutting Farinelli's greeting with a glare. It was a matter of no consequence to the singer. But the snub Charles had received was far more deeply felt. Instead of a royal greeting to a wronged equal, accompanied by unqualified offers of aid, Charles had been treated as a nomadic mendicant and awarded only polite sympathy. It might seem that 'Jamie the Rover' had been succeeded by 'Charlie the Rover'.

With this echo of his father's failure resounding in his mind, Charles hastened back to Paris to review his options. They were few. An alliance with Louis that went beyond hospitality would involve his leading a force to invade Scotland, a strategy rejected by the devious Kelly in favour of an invasion of England, which Louis, in his turn, refused to support. Charles now thought that following his father's policy of gentle persuasion was unproductive, and he decided to take more direct action. He would solve his financial and military problems at one stroke by marriage.

Unfortunately he insisted on a wealthy royal bride and there were very few of these. He had already been rejected as a groom for any of Louis's daughters, and would have to look further afield. His choice was the furthest afield that Europe could supply – Elizavetna Petrovna Romanovna, Czarina of Russia. Aged 39 she was the allegedly illegitimate daughter of Peter the Great, who had suggested her as a bride to Louis but she had been rejected. When her elder half-sister, Anna, had succeeded to the throne as Czarina, Elizabeth took a long series of lovers. The first was Alexis Shubin, a sergeant in the Guards, who paid for his impudence by having his tongue cut out before being sent to a lifetime of exile in Siberia. Elizabeth consoled herself with the bottle – Frederick the Great called her a 'vodka-drenched virago'. Since she was a daughter of Peter the Great, she was a favourite with the army and regularly inspected them wearing full army uniform with steel breastplate. They carried out a successful coup against her half-sister, and Elizabeth became empress in 1741. She was a popular ruler, building extravagantly and using the army as her personal stud farm.

Although she allied herself with France against Prussia she was keen for a rapprochement between France and England. It is difficult to think of a more unsuitable bride for Charles, who expected an invasion force of 11,000 troops as part of the marriage settlement. The proposal came to nothing and Elizabeth died childless in 1762, memorable in the hearts of the Russian people for having outlawed the death penalty throughout her reign.

Charles had another problem that was much nearer home. As always, he had no understanding of other people's private agendas, and his relations with his father and brother were worsening. Discerning the private ambitions of James III and his son was an impossible task, but Charles simply ignored his brother's aspirations and hoped that Henry could, one day, be of use to his own existence.

The two men had been living apart for some time when on 30 April 1747 Charles was intrigued to receive a formal invitation to dinner from his brother. He arrived to find a table laid, a meal prepared and servants at the ready, but his brother was inexplicably absent. Charles waited until about midnight, then left in a baffled fury. This continued until 3 May when he was handed a letter from his brother informing him that Henry had left for Rome some hours previous to the dinner invitation. The invitation had been a ruse to allow Henry a head start of some hours, and his purpose was such that it could not be revealed until he was well on his way. Henry reached Rome on 25 May to receive the news that Benedict XIV had agreed to create him a cardinal at the July consistory. At that time it was not essential for a cardinal to have served as a priest. The wearer of the red hat was simply a prince of the Church, and political connections along with an observance of piety were sufficient qualifications, although the political connections usually counted for more than the piety.

Henry had rightly dreaded Charles's response to the news, which arrived in a letter from James at the end of June. Louis and the French court had known for some time, and Charles had been excluded from the secret.

Inevitably, Charles's reaction to the news was a fit of white rage. He wrote that the news was 'like a dagger to his heart'.

The principal reason for his anger was that the restoration of the Stuarts was now all but impossible. Charles appeared to be unmarriageable, having been rejected by the royal families of Europe – and he refused to consider marrying outside royal circles – so unless Henry revoked his vows of chastity there could be no continuation of the dynasty. If Charles regained the throne, then the heir apparent was not only a Catholic, proscribed by the Act of Settlement, but also a cardinal. Henry took as his arms the Royal Arms of England, but there was an unsolved dispute as to whether the arms should be surmounted with a crown or a red hat. Correspondence shows that Pope Benedict was impressed not only by Henry's piety but also by the £150,000 he was offered by the London Government to grant Henry the office. With restoration now an even fainter hope, Charles had to find a principal purpose for his life.

Although he was, diplomatically, a very hot potato which no one was eager to pick up publicly, Charles was still a figure of high romance – tall, handsome, dashing, with those hints of danger and tragedy that made him attractive to the female aristocracy. There was no denying the fact that the court of Louis XV at Versailles was a dull affair, and the *haut monde* simply set about creating an alternative society.

This was the world of the great Paris salons, each dominated by a *salonnière*. These doughty ladies held receptions on given days of the week, and admittance to these affairs was very much by personal invitation only. Each lady prided herself on the exclusivity of her principal guest and their eminence in letters, learning or celebrity, and the undisputed stars of this galaxy were Denis Diderot and Jean d'Alembert, the founders of the *Encyclopédie*, published in 1751 in 55 volumes. These men were the central figures of a group later described as *Les Philosophes*, one of whose principal members was the Scottish Whig historian and philosopher David Hume, who was introduced in 1763 by his patroness the Marquise de Boufflers.

Such a *salonnière* was the 48-year-old Anne-Charlotte de Crussac-Florensac, Duchesse d'Aiguillon, whose salon was held on Saturdays. The Duchesse d'Aiguillon's husband was the lover of the Princesse de Conti, whose husband in turn, and some time later, would be the lover of the Marquise de Boufflers, Hume's patron. The *salonnières* guarded their protégés with a pride similar to modern football managers protecting their star players. If any of them strayed to a different salon there were bitter recriminations, since the greater the fame and overt loyalty of a protégé the greater was the credit which redounded to their patroness. The patroness was often also the protégé's mistress, although no such relationship seems to have existed between Charles and d'Aiguillon.

Given the political composition of these groups, all severely critical of the *ancien régime* of Louis XV, it was only natural that they should wish to include Charles among their number. It might well be thought that Charles would mix uneasily with the elevated wit of the *Philosophes*, and be granted access simply because of his quasi-royal status, and Charles had certainly displayed a high level of political naivety in the past. However, possibly because of this past career his acquaintance was highly sought after. Also, thanks to the war of the Austrian Succession most male aristocrats were absent at the front, commanding their regiments, and Charles was quite grateful for the opportunities occurring.

He was now entering that dangerous stage of his life when his celebrity was starting to give way to unwelcome notoriety. Nonetheless, he caught the eye of Charles-Louis de Montesquieu, the essayist and political theorist and author of *Lettres Persanes*, a satire on French society published in 1721. He was known for his views on the separation of powers in government, and for the view that while we all want to be happy, which is easy, most of us want to be happier than everyone else, which is difficult. The Prince had written against the rumours surrounding the forthcoming Treaty of Aix-la-Chapelle, and the two men became correspondents. It appears that in treating Charles as a fellow author Montesquieu used the same flattery that Benjamin Disraeli later used on Queen Victoria.

The Prince seems to have been viewed with gentle if sardonically amused indulgence. On the occasion of the British victory at Quiberon Bay in Brittany, which virtually put an end to French seapower, Charles, a guest at the Duchesse d'Aiguillon's salon, unwisely praised British naval expertise. Montesquieu pointed out that the fleet was a Hanoverian one, and therefore controlled by Charles's enemies. The Prince, like all quasi-intellectual but pretentious pygmies, had a quick riposte ready, and simply said that the fleet was his country's fleet and as true ruler of that country he was proud of its expertise. But to the society of the *salonnières* Charles remained politically suspect even though he was socially attractive. Aristocratic and intellectual eyebrows were raised even if his *faux pas* did not merit exclusion.

He was not, however, excluded from the rage of his erstwhile hostess Madame de Sessac, with whom he had been lodging. Now, on a comparatively trivial point of etiquette she peremptorily informed him that his lodgings were no longer available. He was rescued by Louis, who housed him at St Ouen, six miles from Paris. The estate was renowned for its hunting grounds, and Louis was keen that his wayward guest be fully occupied. The estate was part of the property of the Rohan-Soubise family, and on 13 August 1747 the Prince dined with the family matriarch, the Princesse de Guémène, and her daughter-in-law Marie-Louise-Henriette-Jeanne de la Tour d'Auvergne. A daughter of the Duc de Bouillon, whom Charles said he trusted like no other man in France, she was also Duchesse de Montbazon and Princesse de Rohan, so there could be no doubt of her nobility. She was married to the Prince de Rohan-Guémène, whose Jacobite family was close to the Bouillons. She was also Charles's first cousin. The attraction between the two was immediately apparent and shortly after his stay at St Ouen they visited Navarre together. It was probably during that visit, in 1747, that she became Charles's mistress.

This fully formed affair with a regular mistress was an entirely new situation. Here was a highly sexually experienced woman, five years Charles's junior, whose husband was conveniently absent on a foreign campaign. For Charles it appeared to open a fresh door to life for him. According to Marie's correspondence, 'having once tasted the joys of physical love, he soon developed an impressively healthy liking for it'. So David Daiches's view of him in his *Charles Edward Stuart, The Life and Times of Bonnie Prince Charlie* (London

1973), that Charles Edward was not driven by sexual desire but merely had a more than normal wish to be liked especially by the other sex, must be discarded.

In the mid-eighteenth century, a married gentleman's sexual needs were primarily supplied by his wife, who was essential for continuation of the family name. A young unmarried man might choose an older woman past child-bearing age, but most often would take an established mistress. Servants, who had little option in the matter, were available, as were prostitutes, although they were frequently infected with venereal disease. Affairs with mistresses were commonplace but casually indulged in and only rarely undertaken in any long-term relationship. In the past for the Prince there would have been camp-followers, chosen with cleanliness in mind, or presumed virgins taken from captured populations, although Charles is not reported to have used either source.

Therefore, since he had not yet married, Charles would have taken a mistress. Such a woman could simply have been part of a gentleman's undeclared equipage, more personal than a valet but often regarded as more influential than a counsellor. Although their influence would vary widely according to personality and intelligence, in many cases mistresses had more influence than the gentleman's wife. This was certainly true of Louis XV. In Charles's case an instinct for discretion and a noble heritage were essential, and such a woman was the Duchesse de Montbazon, who probably felt the need for sexual satisfaction more than the Prince.

The locations for rendezvous would have been simple to arrange, with both parties being capable of manufacturing excuses to visit. At Charles's house at St Ouen visitors of all sorts passed through the doors, their final destination known only to Charles's footman or valet, whose mouths could be relied on to stay firmly closed. The other possibility was at the de Guémène house in the Place Royale, which the Prince would approach in a darkened coach from St Ouen and be delivered to the Rue Minimes, which gave on to a side entrance to the main house. This system was overseen by Daniel O'Brien, the Prince's valet. But O'Brien was unaware that the whole procedure was under close surveillance by Louis's secret police and he was arrested under suspicion of an assassination attempt. Once the police were told that it was a *rendezvous d'amour*, all was understood. And by October 1747, Marie was pregnant.

Although the affair was just tolerated by the *beau monde*, it caused a split in the Prince's household. William MacGregor of Balhaldy criticised the Irish faction – of Kelly and O'Brien, whom he dismissively called the 'distillers' – for encouraging the Prince's indiscretions.

This reverie came to an end in December when Marie's husband, the Prince de Rohan-Guémène, returned from war, and she was obliged to resume marital relations. Charles now reluctantly accepted that he should not visit Marie until after her husband had gone to bed, and this meant returning to his country home in broad daylight. His coach would arrive at St Ouen at 5 a.m. and 'a gentleman in a white frock coat' would descend and enter the house by a back door. A prying neighbour once approached the coach and was threatened by a pistol-bearing servant. He reported the incident to the police who, knowing exactly what was going on, took no action.

This inconvenience Charles solved by abandoning his house at St Ouen and moving to the Chemin de Rempart near the Porte St Honoré. He was clearly now besotted, with the reckless passion of a first-time lover, to say nothing of a first-time father-to-be, even if he knew that the child could never be acknowledged. Marie reported that Charles would sometimes lay his head on her belly and hold conversations with his unborn offspring, although the excessively late nights meant that he occasionally dozed off, much to the chagrin of Marie.

He was so intensively obsessed that in October 1747 he even discussed rearranging his inheritance so that the de Bouillon family could inherit the Sobieski jewels.

He had engaged Mlle Carteret, one of Marie's maids, to report to him as to her mistress's moods, and she obligingly reported that Marie was frantically in love, to the point of madness, with the Prince. Even among the *beau monde* of eighteenth-century France a limit had to be put on this madness, and Marie was visited by her mother-in-law, the forbidding Princesse de Guémène. She had much greater experience in such matters, and had been told by her own espionage network inside the Place Royale of noises of ecstasy, unnatural in a respectably married woman's establishment, coming from Marie's bedroom. She peremptorily commanded that her daughter-in-law immediately show more discretion or risk social ruin. Instead of discretion, however, she showed folly, confronting Charles who refused to accept any limitation on his behaviour and insisted that he spend whole nights in Marie's bed if he so chose. Marie, in tears, gave in to him.

On 23 January 1748 the Prince de Rohan-Guémène was attending court at Marly, and Marie, now once again alone, was breathlessly awaiting her visit from Charles. Instead, her mother-in-law and father burst into her room and demanded that she immediately write a letter to Charles ending the affair. She collapsed in hysterics.

Her father dictated the letter. It was duly sent but no reply was forthcoming. Either Charles was adopting the inherent Stuart tactic of doing nothing and hoping the situation would go away, or he was paralysed by having to accede to something so against his wishes. On 8 February she wrote again: 'To my dear love. I swear on my life that I would die of joy to see you.' He did write in mid-February, grimly revising his promises about the family jewels. However, Marie persisted in spite of public slights. On 27 April she wrote to Charles that she would be attending the opera and asked him to look at her with 'those eyes which I adore'. They had previously met at the opera and Charles had simply looked away. Charles now appeared at the opera with a lady who was unmistakably a new mistress, thus giving a cruel snub to the mother of his child. In spite of this appalling public humiliation, Marie managed to arrange a rendezvous, and on 18 May 1748 at midnight and in total secrecy the two lovers met in a heavily draped carriage on the Pont Tournant in Paris. The meeting was a long one and we are told that they reconsummated their love. But a great romance thus ended among the sordid cushions of a cramped carriage. It is unlikely that the couple ever met again although Marie continued to pine for her lover. Her child was born and baptised as Jules Hercule, Prince de Rohan and Duc de Montbazon, but died at just five months. Marie herself died on 24 September 1781 in the convent at Les Feuillants. She was 56 years old.

Events on the political stage had moved on as the War of Austrian Succession came to an unsatisfying end. The Treaty of Aix-la-Chapelle was signed in October 1748 between Britain and Austria, and achieved nothing but a cessation of hostilities. Louis had, however, lost a great deal of influence and he was forced to accept a clause guaranteeing that France would cease to give shelter to any member of the Stuart dynasty. He offered Charles a living in Freiburg and was indignantly turned down. Charles haughtily reasserted his position as a guest of France and as regent for his father. He had been offered shelter by His Most Christian Majesty and had taken no part in the dealings of Aix-la-Chapelle. He even had medals struck with his profile on the obverse and Britannia, surrounded by the British fleet, on the other. When challenged about this by the Prince de Conti, he replied that he always regarded the glory of England as his own. Conti noted this as gross ingratitude, but Charles persisted.

He was happy to be *persona non grata* at Versailles since he was still a star in the social whirl of the salons, and none more so than that of the Duchesse d'Aiguillon, who introduced him to Marie-Anne-Louise Jablonowska, Princesse de Talmont, a cousin of the queen. A friend of the Duchesse d'Aiguillon and also in her forties, de Talmont had been one of the greatest beauties of France, with a long string of lovers. In 1730 she had married the Prince de Talmont, ten years her junior and a closet homosexual. She continued to take numerous lovers for her own satisfaction. One description of her states: 'her expression is never natural. She is always posing with her chin in the air affecting now tenderness, now disdain, now haughtiness. She attracts and she irritates. We like her and hate her.' In other words, she and Charles were a highly explosive mixture.

Charles exchanged the exhausting embraces of a passionate 22-year-old for the sexual skills of a highly experienced *femme du monde*. But she was a lady used to getting her own way and she and the Prince were bound for serious collisions. His power base was collapsing as rumours abounded about the imminent enforcement of the expulsion clause in the treaty. Trouble also came nearer home when in the autumn of 1748 the gallant old warrior Lochiel, who still carried some respect internationally, died of meningitis.

Charles's inner circle of Kelly and the 'distillers' would be of no use to him in his search for a bride. He even tried to demonstrate his flexibility of conscience by sending an ambassador to negotiate a marriage with the sister of Frederick the Great, but his envoy was lucky to escape the Berlin court with his life. He also laid siege, unsuccessfully, to Princess Caroline-Louise, daughter of the Landgrave of Darmstadt. Charles had lowered his sights, but again he was rejected.

Predictably there were stormy passages in his relationship with the Princesse de Talmont, who was separated from her husband. Their Paris *hôtel* was unsold and she continued to live in it, alternating occupation with her disaffected husband. This had bizarre repercussions in that once Charles called to see his mistress unaware that the prince was in residence. He was rebuffed by the Prince de Talmont's servants, who immediately locked the doors. Charles, with his usual fury at being countermanded, returned the following day with an army of carpenters who, on his orders, started removing the doors. All concerned risked immediate arrest, and reluctantly the Prince desisted. The Princesse de Talmont had to do what she had never done before, and apologised to a lover.

Charles was now under intense pressure to leave France as the treaty was ratified on 18 October. Having rejected Louis's offer of a refuge in Freiburg, he placed the ageing prevaricator in a difficult position. As Charles saw it, he was a sovereign monarch by Divine Right who, under the treaty of Fontainebleau of October 1745 between his father and Louis, was guaranteed refuge in France, but Louis was convinced that Aix-la-Chapelle had negated any previous arrangement. His foreign minister, Puysieux, sent polite letters to Charles but to no avail. Puysieux then ceased addressing Charles as 'Your Royal Highness', calling him simply 'Monsieur'. Louis had written to James about his son's intransigence, but James knew better than to try to push his son. All Europe held its breath. Charles, meanwhile, ignored the peril of his position and exulted in his celebrity. Visitors came from England just to see him acknowledge the cheers from his box at the opera, unaware that very soon his attendance at the opera would be brutally cut short.

Fresh embassies to Charles achieved nothing, and the threat of arrest evinced the answer from Charles that he would never allow himself to be taken alive. Louis at last managed to get a letter from James ordering Charles to quit the kingdom. The letter was read to Charles, who walked away before the reading could be completed, and he subsequently claimed it was a forgery. The game continued, with Charles almost fulfilling a death-wish as he pushed Louis further and further into a corner, until finally it was decided that he must be arrested and deported. De Talmont had realised that she could have no influence over the headstrong prince, who continued to attend the theatre as if daring Louis to act.

And act he did, on Tuesday 10 December, two months after the ratification of the treaty. The Duc de Biron, the colonel of the grenadier guards, along with Major Vaudreuil and a detachment of soldiers, seized Charles as he entered the opera. He was bound hand and foot with a cord of red silk, then disarmed of two loaded pistols, his sword and a dagger, and hurriedly taken by coach to the prison of Vincennes, along a route already lined with soldiers. At Vincennes he was shown into a cell, he inevitably complained about its size, and was transferred to a larger one. Next day even he realised that the cause was lost, and he wrote to Louis agreeing to leave France with a company of musketeers. He would be delivered to the Pont de Beauvoisin at the border with Savoy. Charles, demonstrating his valetudinarian physique, fell ill at Fontainebleau and his departure was delayed. In the Cabaret de la Poste inn in Fontainebleau, a new arrival was David Hume, returning from a diplomatic mission to Austria. The two men, one an embodiment of the Divine Right of kings, the other a rational sceptic, met for over an hour. Sadly, there is no account of their conversation.

Back in Paris, de Talmont asked to visit him but her request was denied. However, when Charles's lodgings were searched her messenger was arrested attempting to deliver a letter. It was immediately impounded and the unfortunate lackey was thrown into the Bastille. This useless piece of stable-door-locking came to an end when the letter turned out to be simply a sympathetic message of condolence to Charles. The princess wrote to the Comte de Maurepas, chief of the Paris police, assuring him that her *valet de poste* was not personally planning the overthrow of the Bourbon monarchy and politely asking for his free return. There were red faces enough in Paris, as Charles had been a popular exile and a pillar of romance.

Charles was duly delivered on 23 December and rode at once to Chambéry, from where he, now disguised as an Irish officer, took the post-chaise to Orange, then hired a coach to deposit him in Avignon, arriving on 27 December. Avignon was a papal state – a relic of the long-past schism of the twelfth century when the papacy had moved from Rome to Avignon – and Charles's sudden appearance was an embarrassment to the papal legate, who immediately demanded that he leave the city in order to re-enter as an honoured guest. Charles was glad to oblige and to take up lodgings in the Papal Palace.

He made no attempt to make contact with de Talmont but set about establishing his own court at papal expense. Benedict XIV was under pressure from Britain and France to recall Charles to Rome, but he did not want to upset James and Henry, even though it was Benedict's creation of Henry as a cardinal – he had now added to his already lavish income by being created Bishop of Frascati – that had so infuriated Charles, who was now ingratiating himself with the population of Avignon by a series of balls and carnivals. He organised a fountain flowing with wine in the Place St Didier, sending the bill to the papal legate, and started boxing matches and a bull-running, similar to present-day events in Pamplona. This was a particular insult since bull-fighting to the death was banned, but Charles's version slid just inside the law. The pressure on Benedict now increased. Louis was threatening to send the bills for all Charles's massive debts in France to the Vatican, and Britain threatened to bombard Civitavecchia if the pope gave Charles refuge.

Charles had now humiliated both Louis and the pope. As if realising that there was no more fun to be extracted from the situation, he declared himself ill and vanished. Early in March 1749 the news filtered out that he had left Avignon on 25 February for an undeclared destination. For the next 17 years he would lead the life of an international fugitive, now lacking both patronage and money. If the 'flight in the heather' had prepared him for anything, it now stood him in good stead, as secret agents and spies pursued him across Europe from one secret hiding place to another. Three years previously he had been a secret guest in 'Cluny's Cage'. Now his bolt-hole was much more exotic, and it had been prepared for him by de Talmont, probably with his connivance before he left. It was the most unlikely place to search for a libertine prince.

Chapter 11

Charles hid from his enemies in a Paris convent

The convent of the daughters of St Joseph in the Rue St Dominique, on the left bank of the Seine, had lay quarters available to ladies wishing to have an establishment without the inconvenience of husbands, and one of the greatest of the *salonnières* lived there permanently. She was the 69-year-old Marie de Vichy-Champrond, Marquise du Deffand, who maintained a household of two footmen and maids, as well as a secretary who would eventually elope with her most honoured guest, Jean d'Alembert, the mathematician of the *Encyclopédie*. Du Deffand was totally blind but regularly attended the theatre with a companion whose unpopular task it was to describe the action to her in minute detail. Her blindness also allowed her to reverse the day and she seldom retired to bed before dawn, leaving her exhausted guests to return home in the early mornings. She described herself as 'the liveliest corpse in Paris'.

Another apartment in the convent was rented by the Princesse de Talmont, where she lived beside her friends and co-residents Elisabeth Ferrand and the Comtesse de Vasse, all three of whom were regular guests at du Deffand's *soirées*.

Although Ferrand and de Vasse were not related, they always referred to themselves as 'sisters'. Thus de Talmont would have known d'Alembert and Denis Diderot. During Charles's stay in Avignon she had shown some discretion and removed herself to her estates in Lorraine, but now she was back in Paris. Soon she was joined in the convent by the Prince.

He had arranged for his correspondence to be sent under an alias to his banker, John Waters, and on 6 March 1749 he felt secure enough to risk making a collection. He was now living in the convent where there were false walls behind the rooms of Ferrand and de Vasse. The Prince spent the mornings behind Ferrand's wall space, moving in the afternoon to that of de Vasse. The convent was locked up in the evening, when he would climb down a secret staircase to the floor below, which was the apartment of de Talmont. The lovers would then spend the night together.

One might ask what the original purpose of these secret staircases, false walls and hidden doorways could have been when included in the construction of a convent. There were several convents that were rumoured to have had highly specialised and altogether irreligious functions and which operated as little more than female brothels, one of which featured in the novel *La Religieuse*, written about 1780 by Denis Diderot, a friend of the Marquise du Deffand and a regular habitué of the convent of St Joseph.

These liaisons of Prince Charles were highly romantic and not as dangerous as they might seem, since all the ladies involved were well-connected noblewomen, although de Talmont was warned that her maid might well be in the pay of de Maurepas. We do not know whether the nuns of the convent had any knowledge of the liaisons taking place under their roof, but the situation lasted for some months. Charles was enthusiastic about romantic entanglements and was no stranger to danger, but they had previously been brought about by his own initiatives. This was different and the strain was starting to tell.

In the early part of 1749 Charles moved out of Paris, managing to deceive the international authorities who were searching for him, but by November he was back in the convent. He was 'sighted' in Sweden, Dresden and Berlin as well as Paris, Lorraine and Venice. On 11 May he wrote to his father that he was hopeful of being allowed to remain in Venice, but on the 26th he was told to leave. This time he moved to Lunéville in Lorraine, where coincidentally de Talmont had a chateau outside the town. He was offered refuge in Lunéville on the estate of ex-King Stanislas of Poland. He had moved in by 22 September, but by November he was back in the convent playing catch-me-if-you-can with the Parisian police.

In Lunéville he and de Talmont lived in separate houses, since she was more realistically afraid of the Bastille, having recently been threatened with a *lettre de cachet* ordering her imprisonment without either trial or limit of time. Her passion for discretion prompted the outward demonstration of a fatal flaw in the Prince's personality. He had always reacted furiously when frustrated, but now, when she suggested more caution in their visits, he flew into a violent rage and administered a severe beating. He was probably drunk, since his alcohol intake had now increased alarmingly.

This was not the only instance of his violence towards his mistress. On one occasion the Comtesse de Vasse had to remove Charles, physically, from the convent because his beating of de Talmont was eliciting screams that could be heard in the neighbouring street.

He now interpreted her help as gross interference and she threatened to expose his presence. De Talmont was becoming sexually less active and Charles satisfied himself with other *amours*, whom he flaunted as a sign of her incapacity. At other times they would relapse into the old relationship where he called her 'my queen' and she dubbed him 'my king'. The atmosphere in Lunéville became intolerable for the pair, and by June 1750 they were back in Paris, seemingly locked into a relationship of violence and passionate recriminations. She suffered from intermittent headaches, nausea and vomiting which she treated with copious draughts of opium. Displaying all the symptoms of a woman who knew that her relationship was a disaster, she demanded that Charles give her written evidence of his affection. Having been a woman who had conducted her numerous affairs according to her own rules, the towering edifice of her own self-constructed ego was crashing to the ground around her feet. She wanted the ocular evidence of what her instincts could not believe, and attacked Charles for abandoning her. Charles would take his revenge by sleeping openly with a maidservant, and beating de Talmont until the convent reverberated to her cries and he had to be physically restrained. In March 1751 they parted irrevocably at Lunéville, with Charles demanding that his portrait, a present to her, be returned, not to him personally but to his banker, Waters, thus ensuring that *tout le monde* knew that she had been rejected. In his relationships with women there existed not only the explosive violence of sexual passion, either in celebration or in rejection, but also a calculated and sadistic relish in humiliation, which may have stemmed from his resentment at what he saw as his mother's rejection of him in favour of religious devotion.

Charles still occasionally visited the convent as the guest either of Ferrand or of de Vasse, between whom he encouraged unfounded jealousy, but he never again met the mistress of his three-year-long affair. His life was now focusing on what had been his principal *raison d'être* – his claim to the British throne.

First, he asked James for a renewal of his powers of regency, which James reluctantly granted, saying that Charles's behaviour over the past five years in no way deserved such a mark of trust. 'The treatment you give me is a continual heartbreak to me. I send you the commission you want in the hopes it may soon be of use to you ...'

One of the reasons for this revival of interest was the continued illness of George II, who in 1750 was not expected to live much longer. These rumours had encouraged Dr William King, Principal of St Mary's Hall, Oxford, to use the word '*redeat*' (may he return) in his dedication speech of the Radcliffe Camera on 1 April 1749. Charles had also written to Lady Primrose, the queen of the English Jacobites. Through his agents Dormer and Goring, he had assembled a considerable arsenal of weaponry in Antwerp, to where he travelled on 6 September 1750. From there he went to Ostend, where he met John Holker, a textile merchant and, more importantly, a veteran of the '45. On 16 September the two men arrived in London, which event, with the Jacobites' usual incompetence in planning, took their English supporters completely by surprise. When they walked into Lady Primrose's house she nearly dropped her playing cards. Charles met William King and visited the Tower of London, where he displayed what little siegecraft he possessed by declaring that one of the gates could be blown down with a 'petard'. He did not explain how such a mine could be put in place. The timetable for sentry duty and guard-changing at St James's Palace was scrupulously noted. Possibly of more importance to the cause, although of little concern to the Prince himself, he also attended the New Church in the Strand (now called St Mary-le-Strand), where he went through a ceremony of public apostasy and embraced the Church of England. He left London on 22 September and ten days later was back in Paris.

It could be thought that, for the second half of the eighteenth century, Europe was sleeping fitfully as if awaiting the outbreak of the Seven Years' War, which was struggling into life with a long series of colonial skirmishes between Britain and France. A Jacobite restoration was far from everyone's thoughts.

Even Charles drifted in a kind of limbo, half-heartedly pursuing the possibilities of a marriage, first to the daughter of the Duke of Daremberg and then, raising his sights more than a little, the daughter of Frederick of Prussia for a second time. In neither case was his motive amatory, in spite of his new-found interest in the joys of the flesh, but openly in pursuit of a dowry to be expressed in armed soldiers. Neither suit was successful, but the thought was now coming more often to his mind that at 30 years of age, with an ageing father and an avowedly celibate brother, he represented the possible end of the Stuart line.

Others in Europe realised that there could be profit to be made out of Charles's dilemma, and such a one was Alexander Murray of Elibank, a typically cynical adventurer. Through his connections to the Scottish nobility he was a Member of Parliament, although he had caused a violent fracas in the 1751 election and subsequently refused to kneel to beg forgiveness of the House of Lords. For this he spent a short time in prison. Making an advantageous marriage, he gained an income of £3,000 annually and invested some of this in a pitifully small loan to the exiled Prince. It was enough to catch the impoverished Prince's attention and Murray gained admission to the inner circle of advisers. The malign Kelly had long since quit the circle but the group was still dominated by self-seekers.

Elibank's proposal was fantastical and romantic enough to appeal to Charles at first. Two or three (the vagueness is symptomatic) hundred men would lodge themselves secretly in Westminster in order to assemble on a fixed date, kidnap George II and his immediate family, then rush them away to France. All this would be done in secret without raising the suspicions of the army or the Royal Guards, possibly by using their intelligence on sentry-mounting schedules gleaned two years previously, but there was no detail as to how 300 men who could be relied on for total secrecy could be found or lodged. The gates of the Tower of London would be blown open (perhaps with Charles's notional petard) and Charles placed on the throne. Early in 1752 this fantastical plan was proposed to George Keith, Earl Marischal in Paris, who listened open-mouthed but said nothing. Elibank took the Earl Marischal's silence as an endorsement and relayed this misinterpretation to his friends in London. Privately, the Earl Marischal said that you might as well set about capturing the moon with your teeth. At one point the scheme had involved the assassination of the royal family, but Charles overruled this.

Secrecy, never a Jacobite strong point, was impossible. Rumours abounded, while Charles tried to communicate with Waters, his banker, through Elisabeth Ferrand, much to the fury of de Talmont who, when she heard of it by a third party, broke off contact with her erstwhile lover. All communication with England was compromised by the defection of Aleister Macdonell as 'Pickle', a spy reporting directly to Henry Pelham, the Prime Minister. Macdonell had been part of Elibank's inner circle and was still involved in all major decisions, the detail of which he dutifully reported to London, including revealing the date, 10 November 1753, of the planned *coup d'état*.

This lack of security and co-ordination was further demonstrated when Lady Primrose came, unannounced, to visit France, crossing paths with the Marquise de Mézières, representing the French Jacobites and travelling without a passport. Both ladies were under close surveillance. The *coup d'état* was indeed planned for 10 November 1753, and in the summer of 1752 Charles had sent Dr Andrew Cameron, Lochiel's brother, to Scotland to co-ordinate a gathering of supporters who would be augmented by (optimistically hoped for) Prussian troops when the *coup d'état* in London had taken place. There were also strong, if unfounded, hopes for a rising in Ireland with a landing on the west coast of England, and Charles's cache of weapons in the Low Countries was ready. Even Sweden was thought to be poised to come to the insurgents' aid. But this was all talk and aspiration by 'bottle' Jacobites. In cold reality the nearly century-long campaign for a Stuart restoration was finally regarded as over by every-one except Charles.

Frank McLynn exemplifies the frustration of the now bitterly disaffected Highland Tories by citing the assassin-ation of Colin Campbell, a Whig magnate, by Allan Breck Stuart, a Tory renegade. This was the springboard for Robert Louis Stevenson's plot in *Kidnapped*, thus providing us with a great novel and Jacobitism with what proved to be an impos-sible dream of Jacobite restoration, fanned by romance but gradually diminished by reality. Charles had lived with this dream from 1744 to 1752 and now his life would be obliged to take a new course.

His relationship with de Talmont was all but ended and they no longer saw each other. She disappears from history until 1766 when, at 60, she was living in a grace-and-favour house in the Luxembourg Palace in Paris. Horace Walpole, the eighteenth century's greatest gossip, fell over a cat and a chamber pot to reach her bedside. In March 1766 she was still living in devout solitude. Charles wrote to her in 1772 announcing his marriage. She never replied, and died in 1773.

Charles had moved from Lunéville to Ghent in April 1752, possibly motivated by an incident on 21 May 1751, when he had been attacked while on horseback by some opportunistic brigands. He had been unattended and barely outrode his attackers. A possible motive might have been assassination, but a more likely reason for the attack was that the local police had withdrawn their surveillance, since he was now of little importance politically, and as a presumably wealthy émigré he might be an easy source of rich pickings.

According to the Victorian biographer Andrew Lang, 'From this moment the Muse of History would fain avert her gaze from the career of the unhappy Charles.'

Unfortunately, Clio (the Muse of History) was a prying, gossiping hussy and did not avert her gaze. After the failure of the Elibank plot Charles was no longer the tragic figure of Culloden and the heroic fugitive in the heather but was now just another dispossessed heir with no expectations. He took ladies of the *demi-monde* into his bed, and on one occasion even declared himself smitten by one of them, but they were interspersed with increasingly heavy bouts of drinking. This was not the bravado of emptying brandy bottles to shouted Jacobite toasts in the heather, but the lonely sessions of determined sullen drunkenness among disillusioned sycophants. He was allowed clandestinely into the *salons*, rather than being a sought-after guest. Elisabeth Ferrand died in October 1752, severing almost the last link Charles had with the convent of St Joseph, and he was now feeling the lack of a female confidante to whom he could voice his self-pity.

He was plentifully supplied with female bedfellows, but there was no true companion. His mind went back to 1746 when he had been nursed by Clementina Walkinshaw in Bannockburn House. This was where she had promised 'to follow him where Providence might lead him'. Since Bannockburn, Clementina had been determined to take the veil in spite of her family's objections and from 1751 she had based herself in Dunkirk while applying to the prioresses of various convents known to welcome well-born Catholic ladies.

She was now in Douai, a lay canoness yet to take final vows in an order of noble nuns, and in some financial difficulty. Charles had written to her in May 1752 with a gift of 50 louis d'or, suggesting that they meet in Paris. She was held in deep suspicion by all Jacobite supporters, since her sister was lady-in-waiting to Princess Augusta, mother of the future George III.

Considering that his Paris banker, Waters, was threatening to cut off his credit, this was a generous move, but Charles displayed a lack of tact that was amazing even for him, by asking his agent Sir Henry Goring to arrange for Clementina to stay in the convent of St Joseph as the guest of his old friend the Comtesse de Vasse. In spite of his supreme ability to apologise himself out of anything, trying to accommodate a putative new mistress with an ex-admirer was a slight too far. De Vasse refused to comply and sent Charles's furniture and baggage to Waters. Then, with astonishing bravado, Charles invited de Vasse to visit him in Ghent, and unsurprisingly she flatly refused. They never spoke again.

Clementina received with enthusiasm Charles's unexpected invitation to join him and she travelled from Paris, avoiding the convent in the Rue St Dominique, to Ghent where she would now share her idol's bed. But her idolatry had begun when Charles was leading a victorious army. His situation was now somewhat changed.

All this took place before the collapse of the Elibank plot, and Clementina was wrongly suspected by Goring of being a Hanoverian spy. Goring regarded her as a 'bad woman' and complained that he was now being used as a pimp. He wrote to Charles: 'You will despise me for having consented to dishonour myself to procure you a momentary pleasure.'

Sir Henry had reason to complain. His father, Sir Harry, had been the accomplice of Francis Atterbury, of the ill-fated plot in 1721, and Sir Henry had joined Charles's service in 1737 and had been with him ever since. After Charles's arrest in 1748 Sir Henry was briefly imprisoned in the Bastille, but on his release had followed Charles to Avignon and remained loyal. He is a prime example of the group of adherents to the Stuart cause who stayed with Charles in spite of his very damaging, and occasionally dangerous, character flaws.

The great majority of these remaining Jacobites were of one mind as to Clementina, and begged Charles to put her aside. To one entreaty he replied that he did not care for her very much but refused to be instructed as to his behaviour, and would only grant audiences provided her name was not mentioned.

Charles spent the first half of 1753 almost constantly on the move through the Rhineland and the Netherlands, before finally settling in Liège in July. His first action was to replenish his wine cellar. His normal state of anxiety bordering on paranoia was increased by the news that Clementina was pregnant – news he did not receive with the unalloyed joy of a 33-year-old father-to-be.

He was desperately short of money, and was reduced to begging small sums wherever he could, so an increase to his establishment not only of a child but also of the concomitant nurses and governesses, and if the child was a boy, tutors, was most unwelcome. If his lifelong ambition had been the re-establishment of the Stuart dynasty then he might have welcomed the news of the pregnancy – after all, with his first mistress, the Duchesse de Montbazon, he had fathered a son (who died in infancy) five years previously – but his interest could now be seen as his personal claim to a throne for himself.

The child, a daughter, was christened Charlotte in the church of Ste Marie de Fonts in Liège on 29 October 1753. The father was recorded as Lord William Johnson and the mother was Lady Charlotte Pit (both names are probably fictitious). The birth marks the start of the decline of Charles's relationship with Clementina.

On 12 November 1753 he wrote to Goring declaring that he had dismissed all his Catholic servants, and that his mistress had behaved so unworthily that she had put him out of patience, and since she was also a papist he would discard her too. He said that she had told him that she had friends who would maintain her, and other impertinences, so he could therefore abandon her. He also gave instructions that a 'marque' be put on the child, obviously fearing that Clementina might produce other children and claim them as his. However, Charles prevaricated and the warring couple stayed together for the moment.

Clementina's disillusion at the poverty of their fugitive existence can be seen in her words to Andrew Lumisden, assistant secretary to James. She said that before 1745 she had lived in London in great plenty, was between then and 1747 undone, and now lived in a strange poor place, starving indeed.

Much ink and speculation have arisen from the last

sentence. Before meeting Charles at Bannockburn she had lived in luxury, but we know nothing of her subsequent life. Then what happened in the period to 1747 when she was 'undone'? This is usually a euphemism for seduction and abandonment, but by whom? Frank McLynn makes a strong argument for John O'Sullivan, a Major-General in the '45 and one of the Seven Men of Moidart. O'Sullivan certainly knew where she was living in 1752. Goring loathed the man, and when Charles asked him to fetch Clementina he responded, 'let Mr O'Sullivan bring her to you here'. All this speculation, however attractive, is no more than circumstantial, and all we can rely on is the fact of an irreparable split between the couple, with disillusioning poverty and the revelation of a shady past widening the division.

The couple were still together in April 1754, when they found lodging with a M. Florentin in Paris.

There is concrete evidence of the stormy relationship from reports of a row that erupted on 29 April over a totally minor matter. Clementina wanted to go to bed and Charles refused, thinking it too early. The couple obviously lived and slept in the same room, a distinct come-down for a man who aspired to palatial surroundings. Since Clementina was calling Charles 'Royal Highness' between screaming insults at him, the servants and neighbours were easily able to identify the couple. It is probable that at this time she was heard to shout at Charles, 'You may be a Prince, but you are no gentleman!'

Soon their quarrelling became the talk of Paris, but they drew back from parting. Charles was indulging in the Stuart policy of doing nothing and avoiding definitive action. He wrote that his situation was 'terrible, the more that, in reality,

I cannot see any method or appearance of its bettering'. Clementina had found very little comfort, either financially or socially, in her liaison, but could not afford to leave him.

Evidence of their increasing poverty came to light when Charles appealed to Cluny Macpherson on 4 September 1754 to send to Liège the gold treasure that Charles had been forced to abandon at Loch Arkaig on 30 April 1746, but he received the reply that there was precious little left and it would not be worth the trouble to send it. The English Jacobites were now refusing to supply him with cash and each refusal provoked another furious bout of drinking and violence.

When little Charlotte was found to have an unexplained bruise, doctors were consulted who debated operating to excise it. This may have been a benign growth, but more likely the child had been struck a glancing blow during a marital squabble. This was a classically dysfunctional family.

Finally, on 17 September 1754, the threesome left Paris, much to the relief of M. Florentin, who had risked arrest for harbouring a fugitive from French justice. They headed for Basle in Switzerland. There Charles and Clementina lodged as Mr and Mrs Thomson, complaining abut the expense of Switzerland and being forced to dismiss more servants. These unfortunates travelled to Rome and threw themselves on the mercy of James, but he sent them back to Charles empty-handed. The tales of his parsimony grew, as did his alcohol intake, and in September 1755 his doctors treated him for an unspecified malady.

On the heels of the bad news of the missing Loch Arkaig treasure, Cluny himself arrived. He was appalled at Charles's appearance and bitterly resented the accusation that he had purloined some of the treasure, along with some gold and plate of the Prince's personal possessions. He also set about lecturing Charles on his lifestyle, especially on his drinking. It was all a long way from the rollicking drinking sessions in 'Cluny's Cage', and merely drove Charles further into maudlin self-pity.

Correspondence with his father recommenced in October 1754. James sent a request for a statement of Charles's financial situation, suggesting that he abandon his present company and work with James to achieve an alliance with Louis XV who was contemplating an invasion of England. Predictably Charles was livid at this attempt to interfere in his life, and he and Clementina left Basle on another of his secret travels around Europe. James also continued to beseech his son to find a suitable wife, to no avail. In May 1758 the couple were living in the Chateau de Carlsbourg in Bouillon.

M. Thibault, the president of the sovereign court of Bouillon, was deputed by the Duc de Bouillon, whom Charles had once described as the most trustworthy man in France, and whose daughter, the Duchesse de Montbazon, had been Charles's first mistress – to look after Charles's every need, which consisted primarily of keeping the cellar well stocked. The Prince's drinking had reached new levels and, combined with instant violence, resulted in the departure of previously faithful servants, including Sheridan who had been with Charles for 14 years.

In a totally misguided attempt at reconciliation, James dispatched Andrew Lumisden to deliver an ill-judged entreaty of advice to Charles. As we have seen, giving advice of any kind to the Prince was like poking a stick at an already angry bear, and the result was all too foreseeable. James advised Charles to negotiate with Louis, without specifying over what, and reiterated his desire to abdicate in Charles's favour, but without any decision as to when this might be. Finally, he hinted that he knew that Clementina was on the brink of leaving Charles and how pleased he would be, since Charles's various *amours* had badly damaged the Jacobite cause, information that was probably false. Charles's erstwhile adviser, George Kelly, in a fit of pique and wishing to muddy the waters, had previously forged a letter to James, as though from Clementina, indicating her wish to leave the Prince. All this was bad enough, but even more damaging was the fact that Lumisden became Clementina's confidant, and so she became aware of all the machinations between Charles and his father.

Events now moved in James's favour in that Louis encouraged the new War Minister, the Duc de Choiseul, to include Charles in plans for an invasion of England. He was summoned to a secret meeting in Paris, which he attended, totally drunk, and was promised every kind of support. He was offered a landing in Scotland, which he rejected, instead insisting on a landing in England. This was agreed and Charles left for Bouillon certain that he had moved in accordance with his father's wishes and had negotiated a triumph from the French. However, de Choiseul was disillusioned with the arrogantly drunken Prince and had no intention of including him in any plan.

Similarly Charles had no intention of appeasing his father, since he felt that he now held all the major cards. He wrote to the Palazzo Muti telling James nothing of his conversation with de Choiseul, but instead denouncing all his old-time allies, like Cluny Macpherson and Lord George Murray, as traitors. As 1759 wore on and he saw the French making preparations that did not include him he realised that he had lost the game. Predictably, he took to his bed with a supply of brandy.

Charles's domestic situation could not continue. While he could ignore the problem in drunken amnesia, Clementina could not, and as well as protecting herself she had the six-and-a-half-year-old Charlotte to consider. So on 22 July 1760, during one of Charles's unexplained absences, she stole out of the house with her child, heading for the convent of the Nuns of the Visitation in Paris. She left a note:

> Your Royal Highness cannot be surprised at my having taken my pretty when you consider the repeated bad treatment I have met with these eight years past and the daily risk of losing my life. Not being able any longer to bear such hardships as my health being altered by them has obliged me to take the desperate step of removing from Your Royal Highness with my child which nothing but fear of my life would make me undertake without your knowledge.

She went on to assure Charles that she had acted entirely alone and begged that he should not vent his wrath on any other member of the household. The tragic letter gives a clear picture of the conditions she had had to endure and the terror the situation had engendered.

But Charles was genuinely fond of little Charlotte, whom he had nicknamed 'Pouponne', and he desperately wanted her back. He wrote to John Gordon, rector of the Scots College in Paris, that he would be in the greatest affliction until she was returned to him since she was the only comfort in his misfortune. He launched intensive searches for mother and child, using all his contacts from the past, but to no avail. In none of these searches was Clementina mentioned, however. His concern was entirely for Charlotte, although he did threaten, in a drunken passion, to burn down every convent in Paris.

He had always been intensely jealous of Clementina. He was also morbidly afraid that he would be assassinated, so he surrounded the marital bed with tables on which were placed chairs decorated with tiny bells so that no one could approach undetected. The only result of this bizarre behaviour was suppressed hilarity among the servants.

On 8 September 1760, some six weeks after her flight, the frenzy had died down, and Charles received a long letter from his father. It gave no clue to Clementina's whereabouts but endorsed her idea of separation from Charles, although James stressed that he had taken no physical part in her flight. He echoed her wish that she might ensure the Catholic education of Charlotte in a convent. He concluded by telling Charles that his cough had returned. Charles did not reply, nor did he show any interest in the death of George II on 26 October and the subsequent coronation of George III.

On 28 December Clementina wrote to the Prince assuring him of her love for him and giving a progress report on Charlotte, who was reading Latin and French and 'has all the happy disposition in the world and a great desire to write to her dear Papa'. Later, she did write, addressing him as 'Mon auguste Papa', and out of loneliness longing to join him, but not without the attendance of her mother. Clementina ends her letter by waiting 'with the utmost impatience' for a reply. None came.

To Charles's impotent fury, she was receiving 6,000 livres annually from James and from April 1772 was living in some comfort in the convent of Notre Dame at Meaux-en-Brie in Normandy. Thanks to the influence of powerful friends she was now the Comtesse de Alberstrof. Charles continued to receive news through Rector John Gordon including the possibility of Charlotte's marriage, although she was very reluctant to leave Clementina. Clementina's allowance ceased on James's death in 1766, but Cardinal York continued to pay her a reduced allowance of 5,000 livres. Her latter years are shrouded in mystery, but she died in Freiburg in 1802, aged 80, leaving just £12.

Charles was now in the grip of serious alcoholism, hardly eating, and regularly drunk by early afternoon, then sleeping it off before settling down to the brandy bottle for the rest of the day. Apart from his body servants he seldom saw any company and he had become the drunken hermit of Bouillon. Rector Gordon wrote to him begging him to take more solid food but Charles ignored the advice.

He sent agents to Paris to procure girls for him who were delivered to the chateau. Some feared that one of his past amours might travel to Bouillon but nothing came of it. He was now of no interest either to France or to Britain, both locked into the negotiations that would result in the Peace of

Paris, bringing the Seven Years' War to an end with Britain triumphant.

In September 1761 James wrote to him:

> O, my dear child, could I but once have the satisfaction of seeing you before I die, I flatter myself that I might soon be able to convince you that you never could have had a more tender father than myself, nor a truer friend …

Charles did not reply.

Charles was now truly a broken man. His religious vacillations made him a laughing stock, as did his continued drunkenness. Lady Webb, a Jacobite heroine and a rare guest at the chateau, noted that, at dinner in July 1762, his colour rose to an alarming extent, requiring the drinking of pints of water, which the Prince refused to take. More damaging to his ego was his reputation as a man who could not control his women, all of whom finally shunned his company and had departed without permission. Here was not the brave hero of the '45 but the shallow wreck of an emasculated weakling beyond all help, even that of his seemingly much-wronged father.

His daughter, meanwhile, heard the incorrect news in 1762 that Charles intended to marry. He received a tragic letter from Charlotte congratulating him but stressing her destitution and begging that she be received in his court. He replied through Rector Gordon that he would do so, provided that she left Clementina, which she refused to do, saying that instead she would marry some unspecified suitor. Charles, as was his right as her father, refused to give his permission.

His own father suffered a severe stroke in October 1762 which rendered him dumb and partially paralysed. In 1764 he decided that his effective life was over and took to his bed in a semi-vegetative state. This was merely an extreme rationalisation of his ethos of studied inactivity and he continued in this state until his death at 9.15 p.m. on 1 January 1766 with 'his usual mild serenity on his countenance'.

But the calm solitude of Bouillon was broken in 1764. Major de la Motte, the commandant of the garrison, sentenced two outrageously rowdy soldiers to death. Charles interceded, asking for the sentence to be commuted to forced service as galley slaves. This was ignored and the men were hanged. Charles was furious that a mere major could ignore the request of a prince and wrote to de Choiseul demanding that de la Motte be admonished. De Choiseul, aware that Charles was an arrogant drunk, asked that the complaint be made through the formal channels, but Charles had vowed that he would have no dealings with French politics until Charlotte was restored to him, and he did not continue with the matter. He would now have to tolerate watching de la Motte going unrebuked about his daily guard duties. The Chateau de Carlsbourg was no longer a peaceful hermitage.

Lady Webb was still a correspondent for the Prince, and in December 1764 she bravely informed him that, thanks to James's withdrawal from life and his expected death, Charles's brother Henry was keen to re-establish friendly relations. To her joy, Charles replied through M. Thibault that he too would consider such a rapprochement. Henry moved rapidly and granted Charles the pension of 10,000 papal crowns which James would have left to him. Since Charles was now receiving warning letters from Waters, his banker, this was more than welcome. Henry also congratulated Charles on his apparent return to Catholicism. As always with Charles, there was a degree of political manoeuvring in his actions. When James died, Charles would inherit the right to the crown, but it would be meaningless without the endorsement of other rulers, especially that of the papacy. In 1758 Benedict XIV had died and Clement XIII been elected. Charles immediately sent him a message of fulsome congratulation. In 1763 he sent another letter, renewing the compliments and with an earnest wish to keep the correspondence channel open. An element of desperation began to weigh on Charles when in August 1765 Clement suffered a stroke, opening the dreadful possibility that James might die before a new pope could be elected, meaning that all of Henry's machinations on behalf of Charles would have to start again from scratch. So, on 3 October 1765, Charles wrote a formal letter asking for a papal commitment to recognise him as Charles III, King of Great Britain. Henry also looked for support for his brother from Cardinal Albani, who held the curious papal title of 'Protector of Scotland'. The cardinal was a distinguished art collector and lover of the Contessa Cheroffini. He wrote to Charles assuring him of a warm welcome in Rome. Charles, as usual, misinterpreted this as a sign of papal commitment.

Chapter 12

He was a misogynist who tried to strangle his wife

Charles was overjoyed at the news from Henry. Blithely ignoring the fact that it was a promised welcome from one man and did not represent recognition by the Vatican, he started preparations for a journey to Rome. It was essential that he arrive while James was still alive, since on James's death Charles would become the *de facto* king, and Pope Clement would have to either accept him as king of the three kingdoms or cause a diplomatic storm by expelling him from the papal states. He made no hurry to travel and by 12 December 1765 he had only got as far as Paris, where he then delayed until the 31st before continuing. It was a harsh journey with bad weather blanketing Europe. The roads were covered in ice and the passes were blocked with snow. Charles's discomfort increased when Lumisden brought him the news that James had died, at 9.15 p.m. on 1 January 1766, and suggested that Charles delay his arrival. The Prince, however, in spite of his coach having been overturned, pressed on, arriving in Rome on 23 January in an understandably depressed mood which was lightened only slightly by the news that he would be lodged in his mother's apartments in the Palazzo Muti.

Henry at once wrote a long memorandum on Charles's case for recognition which Cardinal Albani delivered to Pope Clement, who said he would ask the conclave for advice. It was clear that he was becoming irritated with the pressure Henry was bringing to bear. Henry then overplayed his hand altogether by publishing all his secret correspondence with Albani, and so lost his support. Albani, following Clement's path, took the matter to a conclave, where it was decided that such open endorsement might antagonise Britain to the point of military action against Rome. Thanks to the Royal Navy, Britain controlled the Mediterranean and could easily commence a bombardment of Civitavecchio, the port of Rome and only 80 kilometres from the Holy City itself. Clement made it clear to the world that, at least to the papacy, Charles was not a rightful king, and as a final insult he had the royal arms of Britain removed from the Palazzo Muti frontage.

Inevitably Charles's heavy drinking continued. Henry felt that his case for recognition might prosper were it not for 'that nasty bottle', which now probably contained Commandaria, the strong sweet wine of Cyprus. Henry refused to allow his brother to accompany him out of doors because of his condition, and Charles's servants were beginning to avoid their master. One lady described him as being 'bloated and red in the face, his countenance heavy and sleepy which is attributed to his having given in to excess of drinking'.

However, Sir William Hamilton, the ambassador to Naples, described him as handsome and good-natured. But Hamilton famously managed to ignore unpleasant facts, such as Lady Hamilton's relationship with Admiral Nelson, so perhaps we must temper his account. Gone from Charles was the habitual lace and finery. His clothes were now often ragged, which he blamed on his poverty, although James's death had left him wealthy. His daily life had become one of increasing solitude, with occasional visits to Henry's bishopric of Frascati where he hunted and played the cello. In May 1767 Henry managed to arrange a private audience for Charles with Clement. Given Clement's intransigence over recognition, the Prince was required to attend incognito and in disguise, a condition that Charles blithely ignored. Clement allowed that Charles could remain in Rome but only as a private citizen. Charles refused the offer but now awarded himself the meaningless title of Count of Albany. Clement realised that there would never be agreement and let the matter lie. It was a goalless draw.

Charles's misfortunes continued with the not altogether unexpected resignation of Lumisden, who complained that his years of bondage had now descended into a form of slavery with the ever-present threat of drunken violence. After Lumisden left Charles did try to give up alcohol, taking the waters in Pisa and Viterbo. By 1769 he is described as being without a blot on his face, agile, jolly and plump. Even allowing for the inevitable sycophancy of subject towards monarch, it was a remarkable recovery.

And then the sun showed signs of coming out. In April 1769 Clement XIII died, to be succeeded by Clement XIV, a Franciscan who was less interested in international politics than his predecessor and who allowed Charles greater freedom. Charles now added Baron Renfrew to his titles. The Prince was now 48 years old and had gained a second wind. He would seek a wife.

Through his contact in Paris, the Duc de Fitzjames, an approach was made to Marie-Anne, daughter of Prince Frédéric de Deux Parts. The rich 17-year-old ignored the request completely. The Young Pretender had lost his gloss as a prospective bridegroom.

In July 1770 he set out on yet another tour of Italy. He was received with the hospitality reserved for the notorious, and he appeared in the Order of the Garter, as befitting a king, and once again displayed his charm to the ladies. This was the perfect remedy for marital rejection. His drinking was now limited to occasional bouts of roaring excess, as opposed to the recent sullen oblivion. The British ambassador in Florence, Horace Mann, a snob of Herculean proportions, confessed that in spite of constant attempts at humiliation made by himself, a world expert in the dark art, Charles Edward was so thick-skinned that he was virtually impossible to snub.

Still in pursuit of a rich aristocratic bride, Charles activated Lord Caryll, who had replaced Lumsiden, and he again contacted the Duc de Fitzjames, who prepared a welcome for the Prince in Paris. Charles, meanwhile, had left Rome, ostensibly for Pisa. He was hotly pursued by Horace Mann's spies, who lost the trail at the Alps in 1771. On 1 September he was back in Paris.

France was still smarting from the punitive terms of the treaty of Aix-la-Chapelle, called in Paris 'bête comme la paix', which had ended the Seven Years' War. Under the treaty Britain gained Canada and India, giving France in return Guadeloupe and Martinique, plus limited fishing rights in St Pierre and Miquelon. The prospect that Charles might marry and even produce a Stuart heir as an irritant to its northern neighbour was very attractive to France, and Louis was therefore keen not only to welcome him but also to provide much-needed finance for the proposal.

Charles at once left for Rome, overplaying his hand by announcing that he expected Louis now to bring pressure to bear on the pope to recognise him as Charles III. This Louis refused to do, while de Fitzjames reported that negotiations with the Princess de Salm and Medinas-Kyrbourg had come to nothing. Setbacks of this sort stimulated Charles to further action, and attention now switched to the princess's first cousin, Louise de Stolberg. Her mother was a widow with the blue blood of most of Europe in her veins. She was the daughter of Maximilien of Hornes and Lady Charlotte Bruce, a descendant of King Robert I of Scotland, and was related to Montmorencies, Crequis, Orinis, Gonzagas and Medinas. She had three marriageable daughters and Louise, the eldest, was aged 18. Charles sent Colonel Edmund Ryan, a French officer of Irish blood, to survey the scene, and he reported that Louise, who had been convent-educated, had a good figure, a pretty face, good teeth and all the qualities which his majesty could desire. Edmund Ryan was also a good judge of horses.

Charles gave Ryan a power of attorney to conclude the marriage settlement. Louise received 40,000 livres annually, with 10,000 livres pin money. Since Versailles was paying, no one commented on the Stolbergs' insistence of extremely detailed inventories of marriage goods, and on 28 March 1772 a proxy wedding took place in Paris. Louise, however, was wise beyond her years and knew very well what kind of marriage she could expect with a near-penniless 51-year-old roué.

When the couple returned to Rome, Charles received two shocks. Louis XV reneged on his promise to pay Louise's dowry direct to Charles, and instead of papal recognition Charles was snubbed by being told: 'Clement hoped soon to grant an interview to Baron Renfrew and his wife, but pressure of work meant that this could not be in the immediate future.'

When news of the wedding reached Clementina and Charlotte in their convent at Meaux, an emotional storm broke out and Charlotte sent out a fusillade of letters to her 'auguste Papa'. None was answered, and so in May 1773, and against all advice, the two women set out for Rome. Charles was horrified but adopted the time-tested Stuart policy of ignoring the dilemma in the hope that it would go away. He let it be known that he would accept Charlotte as part of his household but on no account would he meet Clementina. It was an offer he probably knew she would refuse.

The two women were under threat of expulsion from Rome, but Charlotte did secure an increase in their pensions from both Henry and Louis, showing a determination hitherto lacking in members of the Stuart dynasty. The two returned to a convent in Paris and Charles would never see Clementina again.

Charles, who had moderated his drinking, once more set about emptying Cyprus of wine. Horace Mann reported that he had 'given in to it again as much as ever, so that he is seldom quite sober and frequently commits the greatest disorders in his family'. In spite of this he was often seen in public, at the theatre or opera or riding in his coach with Louise, who continued to behave as a sovereign queen although she was officially styled the Countess of Albany.

In 1774 the dystopic couple moved to Florence, where a weather vane with the symbols C.R.1777 was erected. Louise was at this time in hectic amorous correspondence with Charles-Victor Bonstetten, a Swiss dilettante, who perhaps wisely remained in Switzerland. She was a practical lady – it was she who had managed to get Louis's dowry money paid directly to her, avoiding its dissipation by Charles and saving French face.

Louise was now an attractive woman in her twenties, sexually dissatisfied and highly intelligent. She was also an incorrigible flirt, and while her apologists have portrayed her as an early bluestocking, her biographer Compton Mackenzie pointed out that, in reality, blue stockings are as easily ungartered as any other kind.

She quickly acquired the nickname of 'Queen of Hearts', and her reputation for availability spread throughout Europe. An early lover was Thomas Coke, a young English gentleman making the Grand Tour. The tour involved seeing the artistic and classical sights as well as experiencing the liberalising atmosphere of Europe, especially that of Italy. Dr Johnson declared that no man could call himself educated who had not seen the Mediterranean, and Robert Burns regretted the plight of young gentlemen who returned with 'the love gifts of carnival senoras'. There was a 'hospidale' in Padua which specialised in applying agonising and expensive treatments for venereal diseases, although their cures were ineffective. News of Coke's uninfected dalliance made Louise a popular stop on the Tour – a stop made especially easy since Louise's principal lady-in-waiting was Lucille, Baroness de Maltzan, an ex-canoness nearing 40 of very doubtful morals. Together these ladies formed an erotic hub, all the more delicious for the young aristocrats since one of them claimed the title of Queen of England.

An indication of the grandeur of her court can be seen in another nickname, 'Sultana', and there were suggestions that her hauteur would find easy accommodation in the courts of Constantinople.

The rate of Charles's descent back into alcoholic torpor can be judged by the fact that his box at the theatre was adapted to accommodate a full-length bed so that he could be seen, acknowledge applause, then lower himself from sight to drink and sleep throughout the performance. Louise, meanwhile, was earning her reputation as a bluestocking by reading voraciously and writing countless letters.

She had an epistolary romance with Bonstetten. She told him that he was the man who had captivated her heart, her spirit and her soul, and how she sought a man who loved only her and who knew how to make love to her. On 5 June 1775 she wrote formally to Charles on the grounds that he never listened to her when she spoke to him, and when she complained about the intolerable heat he unfeelingly suggested that she rise earlier. Since she seldom retired to bed until 2 a.m. she objected to this suggestion. This is reminiscent of Clementina's complaints of the Prince keeping late hours at Bouillon. She mocked his reputation as a gallant as he no longer wanted to spend more than a few hours in bed with a young woman who is pretty and who loves him. Sarcastically, she went on to defend herself from blame because the 'Royal Face' is not shining and its beautiful eyes are clouded. Louise also circulated her views to her friends, signing herself as the 'Humble Half of your Majesty'.

In 1774 Louis XV gave way to his grandson Louis XVI, while in 1775 the new pope, Pius VI, also refused to recognise Charles as Charles III. The Prince's health continued to worsen as his bibulous intake increased to six bottles of wine daily – this did not take into account the regular bottle or two of brandy. His growing bulk and dropsy meant that he now had painful suppurating sores on both legs. He slept only fitfully, while snoring loudly. He was also, not without reason, highly jealous of his young wife. He always accompanied her on her outings and made sure that she was at his side while he slept at the opera. She continued to write to Bonstetten, who remained in Switzerland, about the 'unextinguished fire' at the bottom of her heart which 'only he could relight', while waiting for death or disease to walk over the head of her Lord and Master, although 'Thank the Lord the hour had not yet arrived'.

Her need for such release was eased when in the spring of 1776 they moved into the Palazzo Guadagni (now the Palazzo San Clemente). It was not until December 1777 that Charles scraped together the purchase price, at the cost of the Sobieski jewels and his furniture from the Palazzo Muti.

As in 1760 Charles's paranoia about his wife's fidelity resulted in bizarre behaviour. The warning system of chairs with tiny bells attached was re-established, a rearrangement of rooms was made so that hers could only be approached through his, and servants' gossip reported beatings and screaming quarrels, all very reminiscent of behaviour at Bouillon with Clementina. The downward spiral had begun again except that at this time a new actor entered the tragic farce.

This was Count Vittorio Alfieri, a 27-year-old adventurer from Turin. He posed as a poet and dramatist but a serial seducer was nearer to the truth. While passing through England he had fought an inconclusive duel with Lord Ligonier over an alleged affair with Lady Ligonier, although the actual recipient of the lady's favours was one of Ligonier's grooms. Alfieri was a recent sufferer from venereal disease but he was rich and handsome with a demonstrable literary talent. The romantic legend that Louise and he first met when examining a picture in the Uffizi, Florence's art gallery, can be discounted. On such a visit she would have been escorted, probably by her paranoid husband, and Alfieri was too experienced a seducer to risk such a public encounter. He would have known of Louise's reputation and that the port of access was through the Baroness de Maltzan.

She had to manufacture a rendezvous for the lovers, often while Charles snored drunkenly in the next room. This was a fully realised physical affair, strengthened by the fact that at the time Alfieri was writing *Maria Stuarda*, a drama in tribute to the dynasty which Louise now claimed as hers. The comic-opera aspect of the affair came near to changing to tragedy, reaching a violent climax on St Andrew's Night 1780. According to one report, Charles burst in on their love-making, which given the experience of all the characters involved is unlikely. More probably, Charles had celebrated his country's patron saint to excess, even for him. He irrationally attacked Louise, attempted unsuccessfully to rape her and then set about strangling her, tearing out chunks of her hair in the process. Servants at last managed to pull him off, and Louise took refuge in another room where she started to consider ways to effect a separation from her husband and a more settled relationship with Alfieri.

Plans had already been laid with two friends of Louise's, Madame Orlandini and Mr Geoghan. Just a few days later, on the morning of 9 December, Madame Orlandini announced that she had an appointment at the convent of the Bianchettes to be shown the needlework of the nuns. The invitation was extended to Charles and Louise, and they accepted. This shows an amazingly controlled attitude from Charles, who suspected nothing and continued the pretence of marital calm. When the party arrived at the convent Mr Geoghan was waiting on the street, and he engaged the less-than-nimble Prince in conversation while the ladies ran up the steps and rang the bell, which was answered with amazing promptitude. They were immediately admitted and the door slammed behind them. The men arrived at the door and Charles knocked with his stick. After a suspiciously long pause the Mother Superior opened a grille and told Charles bluntly that a young lady had just sought sanctuary from a violent husband and that inviolable sanctuary had been granted. The grille shut again in Charles's face.

That day Louise wrote to Cardinal Henry asking for an endorsement of her actions, and he, backed by Pius VI, suggested that she retire to the Ursuline convent in Rome. She travelled to Rome with Lucille, both armed with pistols, and with Geoghan and Alfieri disguised as coachmen and also armed. By the end of January 1781 Louise had left the convent and was living as an independent lady with Cardinal Henry, who had reduced Charles's allowance and given the balance to Louise. For two years this situation continued, with Alfieri, now lodging as the guest of the cardinal, a frequent visitor to his mistress to make love and read poetry.

Then, in March 1783, at the age of 62, Charles fell seriously ill, to the point of making a will (dated 23/25 March). He had reverted to the Catholic faith 20 years previously and now he received extreme unction and legitimised his daughter Charlotte Stuart as Duchess of Albany. The shattered old man could be seen to be putting his affairs in as much order as his chaotic life allowed.

His brother Henry came to visit him and Charles told him of Louise's serial infidelities. Henry was appalled, and expelled Alfieri from his lodgings. Alfieri left Rome on 4 May 1783 and travelled Europe writing poetry about his betrayal in love. Louise retired temporarily to Genzano, a village in the Alban hills south of Rome, to await developments.

Charles started to recover from his various illnesses and later that year, when King Gustav III of Sweden visited Pisa to take the waters and recover from a broken arm, the Swedish king called on Charles and treated him with great civility as a fellow enemy of France and as an equal king. The two men met frequently and Gustav finally persuaded Charles that all hope of a Stuart restoration should be abandoned and that he should accept the inevitability of exile with the good graces of an ageing king. For the first time Charles was spoken to as an equal with honesty and without servile deference. Perhaps his long-needed father figure had at last appeared, if a trifle late. Gustav also extended his help to end the disastrous marriage, and some historians have seen in this unmotivated facet of friendship the brotherhood of freemasonry.

Gustav was Grand Master of all Swedish freemasonry, and Charles was rumoured to be the worldwide Grand Master. Early lodges were often mainly Jacobite, which is now puzzling given the modern erroneous presumption that free-masons and Catholics are bitterly opposed. Certainly, secret investigations took place during Gustav's visit and specula-tion was rife. But it is all shrouded in a fog of legend.

What is true, however, is that Louise was persuaded to come to an agreement about her papal pensions – she had just received one from Maria Theresa – and Charles regained his rights to the Sobieski jewels. By the summer of 1784 Louise was a free woman and on 17 August at Colmar she was reunited with Alfieri. They travelled for much of the rest of their lives, finally settling in Florence. Alfieri died in 1803 and Louise in 1823. She was 71 years old.

Having been legitimised, his daughter Charlotte bombarded Charles with requests to join him but all were refused. She threatened that since he would not allow her to marry, she would enter a convent. In 1784 he weakened and invited her to join him in Florence. She set out on 18 September. Pius VI, probably to annoy Louis XVI, who had refused to recog-nise her status, accepted her as the Duchess of Albany. She also managed to reconcile herself with Henry who had been frosty towards her. He would have been more than just frosty if he had known that she had been the long-term mistress of the Bishop of Cambrai. He was Prince Ferdinand de Rohan-Guémène, whose elder sister had been Charles's mistress in

1747. Charlotte had borne the bishop three children, the last only a few months previously.

Now she was established with her father in Florence. Charles had been described by Louise as having become an imbecile, which was probably uncharitable, but he now seldom went out as his legs were so swollen with suppurating sores. A musician friend, Domenico Corri, would visit and accompany Charles's cello-playing on the harpsichord. There were legends that he kept a pair of loaded pistols always within reach and had a war chest of gold hidden beneath his bed, but these are no more than metaphors for his habitual paranoia and morbid nostalgia.

Charlotte certainly forgave Charles for his harsh treatment of her, nursing the increasingly frail old man and controlling his drinking. On St Andrew's Day 1784 he invested her as a Lady of the Order of the Thistle. This ceremony, which should have been full of medieval splendour, was carried out in a palazzo in Florence watched not by the nobility of Scotland but by some baffled and indulgent servants.

Father and daughter prepared to return to Rome and they began the journey on 2 December 1785. They were met at Viterbo by Henry and established themselves once again in the Palazzo Muti, where Charles had been born nearly 65 years earlier. The Prince now became more or less inactive, although in 1786 they travelled to Albano to escape the summer heat of Rome, where Charles revived the medieval practice of 'touching for the King's Evil', a totally ineffective cure for scrofula. Returning to Rome, he was now subject to frequent 'fits' or transient ischaemic attacks, and seldom undertook any social engagements. He had, in spite of a chaotic life of gross self-indulgence, managed to outlive almost every one of his contemporaries – kings, popes, fellow rebels and enemies. On 30 January 1788 he died in Charlotte's arms, having received extreme unction from his brother. He was 67 years old. There is yet another legend that, although the actual date of his death was 30 January, the official date was advanced by a day to avoid clashing with the anniversary of his ancestor Charles I's execution in 1649.

The pope would not allow him to be buried in Rome so Henry arranged for a tomb in his own diocese of Frascati, until memories faded and his body was removed to a tomb in St Peter's.

Charlotte lived on until November 1789 when she died of an unnamed illness, possibly a cancer which had been dormant since the first appearance of a lump in her childhood.

Cardinal Henry, now titularly Henry IX, King of Great Britain, France and Ireland, lived on in Frascati until the French sack of Rome in 1798, which saw him stripped of titles and income and cast into destitution. His vast wealth had included lands in France and Mexico, but these incomes also ceased and he lived in obscure destitution. He was rescued when, curiously, a British MP was introduced to him in Venice during a conclave. The MP wrote to *The Times* about Henry's plight and he was awarded a pension of £5,000 and allowed to return to Frascati where he died in 1807.

The direct line of the Royal Stuarts went out not with a bang but with a pair of whimpers.

Postscript

Few characters in history have been swathed in so much romance and remembered with so much misplaced affection as Charles Edward Stuart. But even now, when most of the relevant facts are known, there are still some intriguing questions.

First, what would have happened if he had not turned back at Derby but continued his advance to London?

We have seen that numerically he had a superior force even though the London militia were defending their home city. The Highlanders may have lacked discipline and formal organisation but their ferocity in close-quarters combat would have won the day, and the Jacobite army would have occupied London long before Wade or Ligonier could have come to its aid. With a few well-placed promises of better things to come the ever-fickle London mob might well have accommodated the Highlanders, as had been the case in Edinburgh. Charles's strictures against looting would have encouraged the local populace, and apart from food, drink and women, there were few objects of luxury that held any attraction for Highland crofters. The city would have been his even if his attempts to rectify the most flagrant examples of corruption would have had to wait.

Charles could have claimed the throne, albeit as regent for his father, and with his later flair for apostasy coming to the fore, he would easily have persuaded the Archbishop of Canterbury to crown him in Westminster. But for the Stuarts, kingship was not just a spectacular ceremony, it meant possessing the Divine Right to rule according to the personal will of the God-given monarch. This absolutism had been removed in the Civil War, which resulted in the execution of Charles's great-grandfather Charles I. Since that 'cruel necessity' the royal power had to be endorsed by Parliament. Charles would have had to win the confidence of that now all-powerful body, a power that they had reinforced and increased by the Act of Settlement and the Bill of Rights of 1688, 58 years earlier.

The first fence could have been jumped by Charles changing religions, but this would never have been endorsed by his gloomily devout father, except by his abdicating his claim in favour of Charles's accession. Negotiating new terms with Parliament, dominated by the skilful figure of Henry Pelham, with William Pitt waiting in the wings, would have been almost impossible, and Charles would have been under intense pressure from Kelly, O'Sullivan and the other 'distillers' to form a private cabinet of themselves and other closet sycophants, pressure which in the past he had shown himself incapable of resisting. This pseudo-Jacobite cabinet would, of course, have made sure that the advice given to the Prince was primarily to their own advantage.

Charles, then, would have reigned with a hostile Parliament and a cabinet of self-seeking sycophants. He would have reigned but not ruled. Any ambition he possessed to be equal in power and status to Louis in France, Frederick in Prussia, Maria Theresa in Austria or Czarina Elizabeth in Russia would have been futile. He could not have known that in just 45 years a Bourbon king would be beheaded for absolutism. The present King of Britain had been exhorted by his mother, 'George, be a King!' and had wisely chosen to rule as a constitutional monarch. Such an idea would never have entered Charles's head, thus making it even more insecure on his shoulders than he knew.

Partly, this had risen from his childhood, or rather his lack of one, when he had been separated from his mother by the conflict between her and his father. Both had wanted the boy to be raised as a Catholic but his mother had a level of piety that would have singled the child out for a quasi-priest-like existence. Female governesses were removed since there was a wild rumour that female teachers could lead to homo-sexuality in later life, and Charles was educated in the manly arts suitable to an eighteenth-century prince. His father's court had all the exaggerated pomp and protocol of an exiled monarch, forever indulging in 'state' ceremonies of heraldic origin and no purpose whatever. The entire court lived, lit-erally, in the shadow of the Vatican, upon which it depended for finance. James took no direct part in Charles's education, leaving it entirely to governors who were at Charles's mercy. In imperial China, if a royal son misbehaved, his tutor was beaten and the boy was forced to watch. In Charles's case he was given latitude of an equally indulgent sort, on one occa-sion being confined to his room to prevent him from beating his governor who had overstepped the absolutely random limits of *lèse-majesté*.

This meant that Charles had grown up with no father figure to admire and was reluctant to accept advice from substitutes. Lord George Murray, Cameron of Lochiel and even King Gustav of Sweden were all possible substitutes, but when their advice contradicted his impulses the result was tantrums, which had been indulged during childhood but were ignored when displayed by a grown man. Charles's remedy then was to retire to his bed in a return of one of his many valetudinarian collapses which were, in reality, no more than adult sulks. His Irish advisers were skilful in avoiding these situations by smothering him in flattery and only giving him advice which they knew would feed his already made-up mind.

This irresponsible impetuosity led to his excellence in riding and hunting with bravery and his excellence on the dance floor to the delight of ladies. He also had a bravado in conversation which gave him a reputation for wit and humour. His native intelligence allowed him to gloss over infelicities, such as praising a Hanoverian fleet, and the remarks were forgiven with the indulgence given to royalty.

Thus he grew up in an unfettered atmosphere of admiration devoid of parental influence. His much wiser, though possibly less witty, ancestor James VI and I had been raised under the influence of George Buchanan, a stern, rigorous and totally humourless Latin scholar who ardently believed in regular and savage thrashings. He produced 'the wisest fool in Christendom'. Charles lacked wisdom and was only partly foolish.

He was, however, extremely attractive to the ladies although seemingly incapable of love. His rank and wit were immediate magnets and he knew exactly how to extract continual compliments from them. He became clinically addicted to compliments, and like all addicts became irrational and pathologically demanding when his supply was cut off, reverting often to self-destructive violence.

Discovering the joys of sex comparatively late in life, it is probable that he had little or no desire to satisfy his partners, and the Duchesse de Montbazon complained of his frequently falling asleep.

He had grown up in an atmosphere of discontent and his self-invention had made him the inheritor of this discontent. He set about conquering this by leading the restoration attempt of 1745/6, and when this failed so disastrously he was left with a greater sense of discontent.

His natural lethargy made him approach subsequent attempts half-heartedly. In the tragic words of Caitlin Thomas, Dylan Thomas's widow, he 'had a left-over life to live' without the capability of fulfilling that sad task. On entering Edinburgh in 1745 he was 'Bonnie' Prince Charlie, but from then on it was a downhill stumble through drunken disintegration to death.

Further Reading

Together, three books give an excellent chronological overview of the period:

Mitchison, R., *Lordship and Patronage: Scotland 1603–1745*, Edinburgh University Press, 1983.

Lenman, B., *Integration and Enlightenment: Scotland 1746–1832*, Edinburgh University Press, 1981.

Cobban, A., *A History of Modern France, Vol. I, 1715–1799*, Penguin, 1965.

Bongie, L. L., *The Love of a Prince: Bonnie Prince Charlie in France 1744–1748*, University of British Columbia Press, 1986. Details the affair with the Duchesse de Montbazon.

Daiches, D., *Charles Edward Stuart: The Life and Times of Bonnie Prince Charlie*, Thames and Hudson, 1973. A lively version.

Ewald, A. C., *The Life and Times of Prince Charles Stuart* (2 vols), Chapman & Hall, 1975. An arid and occasionally unreliable work, though thoroughly detailed.

Forbes, R., *The Lyon in Mourning* (3 vols), ed. Henry Paton, Scottish Academic Press, 1974. Letters, memoirs and original sources.

Kybett, S. Maclean, *Bonnie Prince Charlie*, Unwin Hyman,

1989. Useful for Clementina Walkinshaw's point of view.

Lang, A., *Prince Charles Edward Stuart: The Young Chevalier*, Longmans, 1903. The Victorian traditional view.

Mackenzie, C., *Prince Charlie and His Ladies*, Cassell, 1934.

McLynn, F., *Bonnie Prince Charlie*, Pimlico, 2003. A thoroughly sourced and footnoted volume.

Prebble, J., *Culloden*, Penguin, 1961. The definitive work on the battle and its aftermath.